FRUITFUL WORK CULTURE

Prof. (Dr.) Yashwantrao S. Patil

FRUITFUL WORK CULTURE

By

Prof. (Dr.) Yashwantrao S. Patil

Copyright© Prof. (Dr.) Yashwantrao S. Patil 2023

Originally Published in India

ISBN: 978-93-89540-95-6

Published by **RIGI PUBLICATION**
Printer: **RIGI PRINTERS**
Typesetting: **Mr. Shriramchandra Balkrishna Joshi**

777, Street no.9, Krishna Nagar
Khanna-141401 (Punjab), India
Website: www.rigipublication.com
Email: info@rigipublication.com
Phone: +91-9357710014, +91-9465468291

DISCLAIMER

The quotes of various authors used in this book are reverse translations of their Marathi translations. They are not the original quotes.

DEDICATION

Humbly dedicated to

every person

devotedly carrying out

accepted work in his / her life

- Prof. (Dr.) Yashwantrao S. Patil

PREFACE

Dear Readers,

I am feeling really happy to present to you this book Fruitful *Work Culture,* immensely helpful for satisfaction and accomplishment in life. In this book, the word 'work' means any activity accepted to be completed by an individual. Every individual who wishes to make his/ her life happy, satisfied, successful and accomplished would certainly read this book, cover to cover; and certainly make one's life holistically content by contemplating and introspecting on the contents. Each chapter of this book presents a significant approach and perspective about Work. Life will be meaningful if one regards Work as an interesting play. This is precisely what this book attempts to illustrate through various examples of renowned practitioners of thoughts and action, across the world.

When one persists work by intellectually achieving equilibrium of Knowledge, Devotion and Action, life becomes a paradise, shining brightly with grandest happiness, satisfaction and delight. Wholehearted involvement and devotion towards work, finally brings expertise in it. It is then that the best of the innovations is born. This is what the various chapters of this book elucidate.

This book is written with a noble objective of evading the huge possible damage caused to self, one's own family and finally the nation, due to not working, or working half-heartedly, or working with a lack of integrity and passion for work. Certainly, I do not intend to present this book for your entertainment or just to read and to keep aside like a work of fiction. This book illustrates important points in a lucid manner like why anyone would do a work he/she is doing, how to do it, and the like; with the help of motivation, guidance, numerous examples, philosophy, tenets, simple everyday anecdotes etc. The book follows the structure of Principle, elaboration and Summary.

Technology has triggered a rapid change in people's mindsets, tendencies and perspectives. They are changing every day, every moment; whether you like it or not. It is meaningless to waste time and energy in criticizing these changes. On the contrary, this book guides you to accept the situation, utilize the best of your skills and overcome the work problems. Rabindranath Tagore often used to say, 'Wisdom is to light a lamp or to be a lamp to bring light, rather than cursing the darkness.' The same can be said for Work and Work Culture. It does not mean that one may neglect or turn a blind eye to malpractices. One should engage himself or herself with a modest, yet firm, emphasis on the eternal principle of '*Satyam-Shivam-Sundaram*' (Truth-Good-Beauty). Saint Ramdas says,

> "Don't fan the flame of contentment.
> Don't give up efforts. Don't get irritated
> with hard work. Never ever.
>
> Don't leave your inclusiveness. Don't
> be dependent on others. Don't impose
> your burden on someone else."

According to Buddhism, three things can be achieved through Work: A person gets an opportunity to utilize and enhance the virtues he has. He can work in cooperation with others, leaving his Ego aside, and he can produce goods and services required to lead a good life. Every individual longs for transformed surrounding. But, the positive transformation in the Self is a prerequisite for such transformation. 'Walk the talk.' When your thoughts, actions and speech are aligned to each other, everything is possible, smoothly and easily. 'Work and Work Culture' is at the core of all this. This is what the book effectively elaborates in simple, easy and lucid way. Each one of you wishes for happiness, satisfaction and peace in life. I stop here by wishing you all of it through reading and pondering about this book. Amen!

Yours,
Prof. (Dr.) Yashwantrao S. Patil
Cell No. 9890695649

CONTENTS

1. WORK AND WORK CULTURE, AND OUTCOMES OF WORK

Principle: Understanding Work, Work Culture and the outcomes of work is very important.

Explanation: Everyone has to engage in some or the other profession to earn living and to support our family. Even animals and birds are no exception to this. This chapter discusses how to maintain high quality, good standard, integrity and wholeheartedness in the accepted or imposed 'Work'. If Work is a mandatory thing in life, wisdom and happiness lies in doing it with integrity. Doing the work half-heartedly or reservedly is pointless. Anyway you have to spend your energy and time in doing the work. If you do it devotedly, instead of grudgingly, you will attain the true happiness and satisfaction of accomplishment. Work is a vast, multidimensional and interesting terrain. Just like a 'philosopher's stone metamorphoses iron into gold', Work perfects a human being who is otherwise imperfect in many ways. Work gives a real and pure joy. Bertrand Russell, a great thinker and author, says, "A wise, sensible and conscientious man wishes to die while being engrossed in working." Dr Donald Ross, Director of Surgery in the National Heart Hospital, London, says, "Death is not caused by burden of work. It is the lack of work that leads to death." Various learned intellectuals working in various fields have expressed similar thoughts.

A story of Three Bricklayers explains thoughts and perspectives about the accepted work and an inherent tendency to work. It offers us a novel insight regarding our work. Three bricklayers were working on the construction site of a temple. All three of them were asked the same question, "What are you doing?" The first bricklayer answered, "I am a poor man. I am doing this work to earn bread and butter for my family. I am responsible for their sustenance." The second bricklayer said, "I am doing this work to prove that I am the best bricklayer in this country." The third bricklayer said, "I am doing this work to make our temple the most beautiful one in the country." There was a unique shine of happiness, satisfaction and joy in his eyes.

Though all the three bricklayers in this story are doing the same work, their points of view, motives, tendencies and approaches completely differ from each other. Your work or profession may be seemingly more or less important, but it is the motive behind the work that matters a lot. It is your motive that inspires you to work with pleasure and perfection. Those who lack this motive, sense a meaningless void in their life.

Salary or financial benefits cannot be the criteria for evaluating the Job Satisfaction. Let me give you an example. A friend of mine became a law graduate and achieved the first rank in the university. Many people advised him to practice law at the Supreme Court. "You will wallow in wealth. You will eat in a golden plate." They said to him. But, he was motivated and interested in guiding and showing a right path to others. It was a social service for him. He, therefore, opted to become a teacher. There have been many such individuals in various fields, who prioritized their instinct, interest and Job Satisfaction above all, and hence accepted to do a seemingly less important work.

A thought must be always kept in mind: 'Doing work does not mean doing donkey work.' If a person, regardless of his abilities, capacities and understanding, outworks himself/herself thoughtlessly and purposelessly, he/she creates nothing but a mess out of it. Due to fatigue, he/she ends up bringing down the quality of work. Naturally, even a large quantity of work without quality gives absolutely nothing. Bertrand Russell says, "Anyone can be well-settled just by working for four hours. Remaining time can be well spent in intellectual pleasures – in taking and giving it, too." The leisure time, in his opinion, should not be spent in trivial things of fun. Enjoying music is always better than wasting time in playing cards or engaging in gossips. He further suggests that 'cultural aspects are more important than material pleasures. Desire for sheer material pleasures is a vice. A person makes good use of free time after doing a conscientious and righteous work, depending on the person's education, upbringing and culture. If you keep doing a purposeless, unnecessary donkey work, you just waste your life.'

Let's understand the formula of work as it was for the great scientist and thinker Albert Einstein. We all know his immensely powerful equation: $E=mc^2$. This equation has a potential of generating immense energy, and stores in it the immeasurably powerful and destructive energy of an atomic bomb blast. Likewise, he offered an equation regarding work. It is: $A = x+y+z$. A= Success; x= Hard work; y= Play; and z= keeping one's mouth shut. Implementing this very equation, Einstein made discoveries that simply astonished the whole world. He continuously worked hard, and also quietly rested for appropriate spans of time. This is the reason he could make such dazzling discoveries.

Harold Wilson, a successful former Prime Minister of Great Britain, had said, "Six to eight hours of undisturbed sleep keeps a person always energetic and brings great success." We, too, can achieve success in life by applying this formula. Persistent hard work with right amount of rest (sleep) with a peaceful mind are the three keys to successful work. Mahatma Gandhi applied these three keys, and became a great leader of the Indian freedom struggle. If we look back into our history, Chhatrapati Shivaji Maharaj presents a good example of this formula. He lived for barely fifty years. If we skip the 14-15 years' period of his childhood, he had only 35 years of active work. he spent all these years in engaging in war campaigns, fighting battles, and building forts to defend the *Swarajya*. He founded *Swarajya* on the strong base of equality and affinity. It is the same formula that inspired many artists and great personages across the world to reach dazzling heights in their field, which are insurmountable for our intellect. Even if we cannot equal them, we can at least achieve something different, something magnificent in our life by seeking an inspiration from this thought.

Some psychoanalysts have given an equation regarding the effective and successful work. This useful equation is: Effective Work= Time+Method+Capacity.

Time: A person should estimate and control the available time. Every step of work should be completed as per schedule. A meticulous management of the available time is very important. Both work and rest should be focused and unmixed. In short, count time, save time, and work devotedly and on time.

Method: Method of work should be simple, easy, disciplined and flawless. One should be open and ready to make relevant changes, bring improvements and accept new ideas.

Capacity: All your capacities and abilities should be collectively utilized while working. It is necessary to be persistent while working, without getting depressed and losing hopes due to failures. Accept Work as a companion of life.

Suffering is an inevitable part of human life. It is as inevitable as death. However, wisdom lies in confronting the painful incidents with conscience, courage and patience. Your ultimate well-being lies in not losing your peace of mind. When Saint Gadagebaba was engrossed in *keertana*, he received a note informing him of the sad demise of his son. He read the note and kept it aside. 'He simply passed on, just like he had come. Why to lament on it?' said he, and resumed the *keertana*. With a calm and focused mind, he guided thousands of people for almost two hours, on maintaining hygiene, getting rid of superstitions, educating their children, so on and so forth.

Therefore, one should always be thoughtful, active and persistent. Everyone wants to achieve 'self-actualisation'. But, an aspirant of self-actualisation should consider work as meditation; he should immerse himself in the work. He should be ready to take responsibilities independently. He should be always active, without compromising with values, standards and quality. An approach of 'work is worship' is useful. A self-actualised person attains bliss through nothing but work. M. Vishweswarayya is an excellent example of a self-actualised man. He was a saintly person who always strived for people's welfare. When asked about the secret of his 'long' life and his colossal work, he answered, "It became possible only because of relentless hard work, disciplined life, meagre luxuries, and a satisfied and happy mindset."

Summing up: Work must be the first priority among various things one has to do in life. Work can fulfill all the needs of a person and his family. Food, cloth, shelter, education and health are the fundamental needs of every individual. They need to be fulfilled in order to lead a quality life. They can be fulfilled only through Work and Work Culture.

***

2. ANT AND THE GREAT DELUGE

Principle: Always being active is a sign of diligence.

Explanation: There was a period in my childhood when people in and around our village had only one topic to discuss: 'The Great Deluge'. We, school-going children, were frightened by this talk. The world will be drowned! There will be a Great Deluge!! We all will perish with it! We would ask each other in anxious tone, "When will this Great Deluge happen?" Very soon. On the coming new moon. Everywhere people were discussing it, and we were baffled by the talk. Poor helpless children as we were, we were frightened and anxious.

One day, we gathered courage and approached our teacher, Mr Joshi, who was a strict disciplinarian. We asked him, "Sir, when will this Great Deluge come? And what will happen then?" Our teacher asked us to stop our noise, and said, "Dear students, there will never be such a thing like the Great Deluge. And even if it happens, you and I, all are going to have a great fun!"

"How, Sir?" We were so surprised that we all asked him together. He firmly stared at us and said, "You won't have to study. No trouble of memorizing tables. No trouble of writing dictation. No bother of all these inkbottles, pens, slates, books and everything else. No one will scold you for not memorizing tables, nor anyone will punish you for not writing dictation. Won't it be a great fun?" While our teacher was telling all this, the bell rang to signal that the school was over. We immediately flew off and came home. We threw our schoolbags away. We won't have to study. We won't have to memorise tables. We won't have to write dictation. In short, we can have fun; there will be ample time to play without even the least botheration of anyone. We were ecstatic by these thoughts. My grandmother sensed my ecstasy.

Overwhelmed with delight, I asked my grandmother, "Granny, what is meant by the Great Deluge? When will it happen?" She cuddled me and patted my back, "There is no such thing as the Great Deluge, my child. It will never happen."

"No Granny, it *will* happen. All my friends, even my teacher said that there will be the Great Deluge. Only you are saying that it won't happen." I said grumpily. Granny asked looking at me with amusement, "Okay, suppose it happens, what is the use to you?" "You know, Granny, if there is the Great Deluge, we all can have great fun." I enthusiastically told her. She was yet more amused. She asked, "How can you have a great fun?"

"You know nothing at all, Granny. We won't have to do any work." I told, pitying the ignorance of my grandmother. "What do you mean?" Granny asked and lovingly pulled me towards her.

"There will be no study, no tables to memorise, no dictation to write, nothing at all. No scolding by Joshi Sir, no punishment. Then we will be free to play and enjoy and chitchat whole day." I was as ecstatic as a river flowing jumpily across rocky regions. Finally, Granny said after her patience met its end, "I can tell you when there will be the Great Deluge." I, full of curiosity, cuddled her and said impatiently, "Yes, do tell me, Granny." She gently pushed me aside, and said, "Listen, if you find a resting ant anywhere near house or in the yard, tell me immediately. Then I promise to tell you when the Great Deluge will happen."

The task given by Granny appearedto me very easy. I immediately went out to search for a resting or sleeping ant. I tried to look for an idle ant in the yard, near the roots and branches of trees and bushes, beside small anthills, wherever possible. I simply forgot hunger and thirst in this task. But I could not found at all an idle, resting or sleeping ant.

Eventually I told my grandmother, "Granny, as you told, I looked everywhere for a resting and sleeping ant, but I found it nowhere. I accept my defeat. Please tell me now, when will the Great Deluge happen?" I pleaded with her and hugged her.

"Ants have a reputation for disciplined and unending work. Every moment, they are busy doing some or the other work. Even the distribution of their work is fixed. Infertile ants collect soil particles, and build anthills where all ants can stay and store their food. Some ants collect food whereas some others look after maintenance and other works. So, when you find an ant resting, playing, enjoying or sitting idle, the Great Deluge will happen. Got it?" Granny told me, admiring the industrious nature of ants.

Being a child, I could not understand much then, but now I know the importance of work. Just like ants, most animals have to work for getting food and shelter. Honeybees, butterflies, all other animals and birds work. Charles Darwin, the Father of the Theory of Evolution, wrote his last book on earth worms. He invested forty years of persistent research in writing this book. Eventually he proved that earthworms bring 18 tons of soil per acre of the Chalk Hills in Downs (England). How exemplary work does a small creature like earth worm! So is the work of other tiny insects and worms. We human beings are different from the rest of the animal kingdom. We are better-off than they are. Work is an inseparable part of our lives. A psychologist like Maslow says, "The features of an individual's personality are indicated by the excellence and high quality of the person's work. One can understand a personality through the work of that individual."

Summing up: Persistence and engrossment in the accepted work is a distinguishing feature of a sublime personality.

***

3. WORK: BANISHMENT OF BOREDOM, VICES AND PAUCITY

Principle: Do not expect to get something without doing any work.

Explanation: Ganesh, Nagesh and Santosh went to a 'Guru's' *aashram* called *'Ichchhapurti'* to attain peace of mind and energy to work. All three of them were well-educated and healthy guys. But they had developed nonchalance in the peak of their youth. They were infatuated by objects of pleasure and enjoyment. They wanted to achieve something magnificent, but without doing any work and without getting into any occupation. Therefore they went to the Guru's *'Ichchhapurti' aashram* to see him and get some guidance from him. Their only intention in entering the *aashram* was to receive an initiation into *'Sahaj Utkarsha Samadhi'* (Easy Prosperity Meditation). Since many celebrities used to frequent this *aashram*, they had got attracted to the place.

They had heard that one can be prosperous and fulfil all wishes just by applying sandalwood paste on forehead in a particular manner. Having faith in this heresy, they had arrived at the *aashram*, without bothering to give a logical thought to it. Some days passed, and they attained nothing butgetting the sandalwood paste applied on their foreheads. They were frustrated instead attaining positive energy and fulfilment of desires. They began to sense that prosperity does not come as a result of any initiation, sandalwood paste and the garlands around neck and rings in fingers. People in the *aashram* used to always say, "Everything will be fine. You will be prosperous very soon. Have patience… keep meditating." They had to pay certain amount to the Guru as the offering which they used to pay ungrudgingly. They were paying money to the *aashram* in pursuit of their mirage-like hope to attain happiness and satisfaction and to get rid of their frustration, laziness and paucity. However, they understood within a few days that they were being cheated by the Guru in the *aashram*. In a raid, drugs were found in the *aashram*. Involvement of many celebrities in this scandal was proved. The three friends now understood what kind of peace of mind these celebrities were seeking in the *aashram*. They determined to leave the place, and one day, they fled away, evading the strict vigilance around the *aashram*.

Coincidentally, just outside the *aashram,* they met one of their classmates – a bright, clever, hardworking and studious girl called Sanjeevani. They used to know each other since they had completed their higher education from the same college. After having a small talk, Sanjeevani invited the three friends to the farm of her foster father, her greatest support. The three friends, anyway, were in no hurry. They accepted Sanjeevani's invitation.

Sanjeevani's foster father was relaxing under the soothing shade of a mango tree in his grove. Despite being very old, his face was glowing with a soothing calm, satisfaction and happiness. The enthusiasm, happiness and glow on his face outshined that on the face of Guru in *Ichchhapurti aashram*.

Sanjeevani touched her father's feet in reverence, and introduced the three friends to him. He cordially welcomed them. He asked Sanjeevani to bring a *kambal*, a ragged woollen rug from their humble cottage, and all of them sat on it. They started chatting with each other. To the three friends, this farm seemed more soothing and serene than the magnificent corporate *aashram*. The *kambal* they were sitting on felt much more comfortable than the opulent red velvety carpet in the *Ichchhapurti aashram*. After relishing fresh fruits, Ganesh asked the old man, "Sir, you may be knowing a lot about the neighbouring *Ichchhapurti aashram*, don't you?" The father said, "I don't know much about the *Ichchhapurti* or whatever *aashram* you are talking about. I never tried to know more about it, either. I and my family are so busy working on my farm that I hardly get time to enquire about it. Rather I don't feel the need at all."

The three friends were amazed by his simple, stoical answer. They were slightly ashamed as well. "You may have to do too much hard work here, don't you?" They asked the farmer with a surprised admiration for the farm full of green crops and fresh flowers and juicy fruits.

"Oh, not at all! We all work in our farm for our own happiness. For us, work is like some favourite play, where no one pressurises us. Our work in the farm is delightful play for us. It's our pleasure. Even Sanjeevani works with us on holidays. It's a real enjoyment to work. Now it has become a delightful part of our life. Since I am aged now, my family doesn't let me work much." The old man was telling in a very contented tone. The three friends were learning the motivating philosophy from the old farmer.

"How is it that Sanjeevani is your foster-daughter?" asked Santosh. "It's a long story. I had three sons. But we wanted a daughter. So I adopted a girl from an orphanage, when she was a baby. Even the people at the orphanage don't know the whereabouts of her parents. Now we are her parents. She is the beloved sister of my all three sons. She is the apple of our eye." The foster father was speaking with satisfaction.

"Come, boys, Let's have a stroll around the farm." He told them, and all went to have a stroll. "God created us all to work honestly; not to waste life in fun." Listening to the words of the old farmer, the three boys felt ashamed and exchanged knowing glances among each other. "Boys! You are young. You have a tremendous energy to work. Remember, *Ichchhapurti,* or the fulfilment of desires, or the realisation of goals is not possible without Work. You can attain nothing by visiting *aashrams,* and wearing garlands around neck and rings in fingers. It is simply a neurosis to imagine such things without doing any work."

Meanwhile, Sanjeevani too came and joined them. "Dad was a professor of Philosophy in the city. He has done M.A. in English. He decided to come to this to doan action research on the lives of farmers and labourers. You know, Carver and Mahatma Gandhi always told – 'Go to village, stay there, work hard'. Dad's choice of this field was a conscious decision. He left all the so called luxuries behind.   Right, Dad?" While narrating all this, Sanjeevani's eyes were filled with admiration for her father. But without minding and getting carried away by this praise, the old man said, "Every individual's mind is like a deep cave where Satan lives is hiding. It is Satan who germinates vicious tendencies like laziness, loafing, desire to get easy luxuries, and so on. It is only Work and the industrious nature that frees the individual from this Satan. No human being is perfect. Neither am I. But an individual can reach heights of progress if he gets freedom, nutritious food, and nice work to do. After all, it is a person's self-reliance that helps him attain the true happiness and satisfaction. A psychologist named Eric Fromm draws a conclusion on the basis of his research: an idle person gets bored, and eventually turns cruel and violent. Therefore Work is the only panacea for these problems." All of them including Sanjeevani were delighted and amazed to listen to his words. They bowed and touched his feet in reverence, because they had seen in him a glimpse of true divinity. Now it was the lunch time, hence they went into the humble cottage to enjoy the deliciously simple meals.

Summing up: 'Work' is the only remedy to banish your boredom, vices and paucity. It is the pathway to true and pure happiness.

***

4. IDOLS OF 'SELF-ACTUALISATION'

Principle: If the accepted work is performed with integrity and dedication, it gives a contentment of self-actualisation.

Explanation: Most of the people have innumerable needs and wants. Everyone works in order to fulfil them. A starving person can think of nothing but a way of getting something to eat. He cannot think of love or other emotions at that moment. It happens because food is the primitive need of everyone – here, the concerned person. However, when this need is fulfilled, when stomach is full, the person starts thinking of love and other emotions. It is Work that can satiate all your emotions except the familial love. Therefore, 'work' is as essential for life as food or water. Else, emptiness will devour you, and arouse you to get engaged in unwanted activities. Hence, eventually, Work is more significant than anything else. A person can attain the goal of life or 'self-actualisation' through work. Hence work is the soul of self-actualisation.

The fundamental needs such as food, clothes, shelter, health and education can be fulfilled only through Work, because it generates money required to fulfil these needs. A successful individual is characterised by working to attain 'self-actualisation', instead of doing the work half-heartedly. Self-actualisation in work simply means 'to develop your inherent qualities to an optimum level, and to bring excellence to the work you are doing, with the help of these qualities.' This is a never-ending process. There is no halt in it. Stephen R. Covey's book *7 Habits of Highly Effective People* gives powerful lessons for self-development. Reading and contemplating over such booksis therefore highly beneficial.

A person working towards self-actualisation can be described as follows: the person who aspires for self-actualisation, regards his/her work sacred and is engrossed in it. Such a person is always ready to accept responsibility. He/she gives a deep thought to the accepted work; gives prominence to the values and principles while working. He/she is open-minded and tries to understand others. His/her thoughts, deeds and behaviour are simple, straightforward and extremely natural. Since these people do not let any negative thoughts in their mind, they are always enthusiastic and magnanimous. They firmly believe in 'their work being the most sacred thing on this earth.' Work is some enjoyable play for them.

Douglas Bader is an inspiring and excellent example of a self-actualised person. He was a fighter squadron leader in the World War II in which he had lost both his legs. In 1928, he was recruited in the Royal Air Force. In 1931, his plane crashed while demonstrating a drill, and he lost his legs in the horrible mishap. The Royal Air Force arranged to fit artificial legs to his body. He took great efforts learning to be able to walk with the help of his artificial legs. In 1941, he was promoted on the post of Wing Commander. He defeated fifteen enemy planes.

In August 1941, the enemy attacked his plane and arrested him. One of his artificial legs got damaged. Yet, he showed exemplary courage even while being a war prisoner. He used to continuously attempt to run away. During the victory celebrations, he was made leader of the Spitfire planes division. Several handicapped people got inspiration from his story and his tendency of working relentlessly. He overcame fatal and severe problems in his life and achieved unparalleled success. This is why he is an inspiring example of an aspirant of self-actucalisation. The person who wants to attain self-actualisation must continuously learn through such examples and get inspiration from them.

Another example of a self-actualised personage is M. Visvesvaraya of India. He was a modern-age ascetic personality who constantly worked for the welfare of people. He spent his entire long life serving our nation. Once he was asked about the secret of his long life. He said, "relentless work, constant activity, disciplined lifestyle, meagre luxuries, and satisfied and optimist mind and actions." He was a dynamic engineer. Later he also earned reputation as an innovative and efficient administrator. He invented a variety of machines. He started modern methods of irrigation; built automatic doors for dams. When he was the *Diwan* of the Princely State of Mysore, he brought multifarious development to Mysore. He became renowned as an innovative architect of Mysore. It was the outcome of his constant activeness and self-actualised mind.

'Produce or perish!' was the motto of his work. He had a great fondness for perfection and accuracy. He regarded all works as sacred. He always used to say, "Even if you work as a so called ordinary sweeper to clean the roads, you should be determined that the road you swept would be the cleanest and neatest one in the world." He hated clumsiness in work, procrastination, tendency to do inaccurate work. He always insisted on meticulous utilisation of time. He was a very kind-hearted, yet a disciplinarian administrator. He emphasized a hundred per cent accuracy in work. Although he had a very sharp memory, he never depended on it. He always used to verify all details and statistics. His dress used to be as clean and neat as his work. Even if he worked for a whole day, not a single blot of dust used to be there on his clothes.

He was a man of principles and had an exceptionally spotless character. Those days, there was no electricity. People used to work in the light of candles. M. Visvesvaraya would use official stock of candles only for official work. As soon as he started his personal work, he would use his own candles. When he resigned from his post of the *Diwan* of Mysore, he returned home in his private car. He was never partial in recruiting or promoting anyone. There was only one criterion that he knew: quality of work. Just like him, many well-known personages have worked in various fields and have achieved self-actualisation. They left their everlasting imprint on their respective areas of work.

There are many people around us who perform so called trivial or ordinary jobs for us. For instance, newspaper boy, vegetable seller, or fruit vendor, housemaid or cook, farmer, farm labourer, teachers in schools and colleges, engineers… whoever the person may be, when he/she works towards self-actualisation, it ultimately leads to everyone's welfare. This is the reason that self-actualisation has so much prominence in Work Culture. It is this inspiring culture of work that shapes and builds an individual, a family, society and nation. These idols of self-actualisation will keep guiding you like a lighthouse. It is a blessing to bathe in the light of their inspiration.

Summing up: Every person born in this world will die one day, but while living, it is important to learn lessons of self-actualisation. These lighthouses of the past and the present will guide you.

***

5. WORK, AND THE AESTHETICS OF WORK

Principle: Accuracy, quality, and the feeling of 'self-actualisation' in work endows it with beauty.

Explanation: Everyone craves for beauty and an aesthetic experience. Such an experience gives a great delight as well as a vibrant energy. Beauty creates a serene and happy ambience. In other words, beauty fuels enthusiasm that in turn promotes work. It does not let you be bored of work. Those who perform their work neatly and beautifully can always experience the bliss of self-actualisation and the beautiful ambience of work. Beauty in work is an indirect source of encouragement for work; it promotes enthusiasm in work.

Many reputed organisations, companies, offices and banks give a specialised and scientific thought to Capacity Building. They seek expert suggestions and guidance in this regard, and make relevant changes from time to time. In case of work, those who accept these changes can achieve prosperity and progress; those who do not, either lag behind or perish.

Once there was a cloth merchant called Gunidas. He, through his truthfulness and honesty, had prospered in his business. Now he had become old. He decided to hand over the business to his twin sons, Ram and Shyam. He called them near to tell them what he was thinking. He wished they should sell the old shop, get equal share of the money, and invest it in textile business. He had already purchased two shops of equal area in the centre of the city. Both his sons, conceding to their father's wish, started their own businesses there.

Shyam attractively decorated the interior and exterior of the shop. Despite being a humble shop, it had a serene, pleasing ambience that attracted customers. Salespeople in the shop were soft-spoken, courteous and used to display clothes to the customers till they were satisfied. Shyam had specially trained them. Even the cashier had a smiling face and was very prompt in his work. Shyam's shop soon became famous in the city as well as in surrounding suburbs and villages. It earned reputation for the reasonable rates, good quality products, and an excellent, polite and customer-oriented service. A framed photograph was displayed near the entrance of the shop, just above the cash counter: it was a smiling photograph of his late father Gunidas Agarwal. Every morning, he used to offer a garland of fresh, aromatic flowers to his father's photograph. There was a board displayed in a central place which would attract everyone's attention, with these words written on it: 'Customer is God'.

Ram had also set up his shop nicely, but he lacked the beauty, ease and relevance. The service in his shop failed to attract the customers. It lacked cleanliness and neatness. Salespeople in his shop were unenthusiastic and bored. A framed photograph of his late father, Gunidas Agarwal, was displayed in his shop as well, but it was never cleaned, nor was any garland offered to it. A board placed in the centre of the shop read, 'Our satisfaction lies in the customer's satisfaction.' However, the service in his shop was far from giving any satisfaction to the customers. Cleanliness, neatness, customer-oriented approach and hospitality are the soul of a cloth shop, and it was precisely what was missing in Ram's shop. Naturally, customers did not prefer his shop despite its being at a vantage point.

Everyone, including children and adults alike, has a fascination for beauty and neatness. Everyone craves for beauty. These two shops were no exception to it. It is the aesthetic sense and corresponding action that leads to the development and prosperity. Japanese people have a craze for perfection, beauty and cleanliness. This craze is the secret of their progress and development. They have a very fastidious aesthetic sense. They are inclined to perform their work beautifully, neatly, attractively and accurately—may it be however trivial or important. George Mikes, in his book *The Land of the Rising Yen*, describes how neatly they pack even the garbage: "In Japan, there was a huge pile of garbage behind a factory. It looked captivating just like a mountain. The garbage was not scattered everywhere. It was classified as wet and dry garbage. The bags were tied with neat knots, and they were piled upon each other neatly, just like a pyramid. That part of the city was scattered with such small or big beautiful pyramids, and it was looking beautiful."

I witnessed a simple example of the beauty and neatness in work. A friend of mine is a writer. He has hired a middle-aged assistant who manages his office, library, as well as types the content, sends letters, prepares typeset copy of the content as told by my friend, keeps the study-room and library neat and tidy, and looks after correspondence. Once, this assistant suddenly went on a long leave.

One of my students, who was a graduate and had good knowledge of computer, was in need of a job. She had already told me so. I recommended her to my writer friend to hire her temporarily. Although reluctant whether she will be able to manage the work, he hired her respecting our friendship. But she made the best of this opportunity, using her aesthetic sense and diligent nature.

Firstly, she made my friend's writing table, entire study-room and the library as clean as a mirror. She kept all the scattered files, papers and books in order, arranging them well. She neatly arranged computer, printer and other devices. She started keeping a vase of fresh fragrant flowers on his writing table; kept pens, pencils and other material in place; kept a bunch of papers for him to write on. She had perfectly understood what my friend expected. She did everything for my writer friend that she would have done for her own father.

One day, I paid him a casual visit. He was in a very happy mood, and was engrossed in writing his new book. I think he was working on the tales of inspiring Work Culture. His mind was filled with serenity. He could easily find the books and references he needed. The girl was typing the content on the computer. The whole ambience was very fresh, work-friendly and motivating. My friend was very happy with the accuracy, aesthetic sense and vibrant positivity of the girl's work. He hired her permanently, instead of hiring her temporarily as he had thought earlier. She decided to get further education while working for him. My writer friend had decided to extend all necessary support to her.

If a person makes his mind, he can always find a better and more beautiful way of doing every small or big work. It gives a unique pleasure and satisfaction. No matter which field you work in or what kind of work you do, your aesthetic sense and accuracy always prove beneficial for you as well as others. It fills your existence with a new vibrancy every day. You can experience the nobility, happiness and satisfaction in work. You can get rid of physical and mental fatigue. Beauty in work can make you experience the meaningfulness of life. You get a right direction of life. You get happiness and satisfaction of self-actualisation. Fernand Leger, a renowned artist, says, "People are in need of more beauty than we can think of. Right from children to adults, every human being craves for beauty. This passion for beauty lies behind almost three fourth of our expressions and desires."

Lord Mountbatten used to do his work with an enthusiasm, neatness and aesthetic approach. When he first came to India as the Viceroy, he had to interact with many people so that he could understand the situation in the country. He conducted these interactions in an innovative way. It resulted in his own happiness as well as that of the assisting officers, helpers and interviewees. Aesthetic approach and systematic manner of work uplifts the quality of work to new heights.

Summing up: An aesthetic sense in work and actions enhances the quality, merit, ease and happiness in work.

***

6. WORK: METHODS AND APPROACHES

Principle: The best outcome of Work is determined by the objective behind, attitude towards and method of working.

Explanation: In this vast world, some or other work keeps going on in various countries, cities, villages, families, factories, offices and so on. A great variety and vast difference is found in approaches and objectives in works and in people doing those works. Though it is the reality of work, the insistence on the noble attitude towards work, inclusive objectives and the fundamental principle of *Satyam-Shivam-Sundaram* (Truth-Good-Beauty) is always superior and beneficial.

A question was asked to the bricklayers working on the construction of temple, "What are you doing?" The first bricklayer answered, "I am a poor man. I am doing this work to earn bread and butter for my family. I am responsible for their sustenance." The second bricklayer said, "I am doing this work to prove that I am the best bricklayer in this country." The third bricklayer said, "I am doing this work to make our temple the most beautiful one in the country." There was a unique brilliance, happiness, satisfaction and joy in his eyes.

All the three bricklayers were doing the same work; but their points of view, motives, tendencies and approaches are completely different from each other. Whatever small or big, more or less significant work you may do or profession you are in, it is the motive behind the work that matters a lot. It is this motive that inspires you to work happily and perfectly. Due the lack of this motive, many people sense a meaningless void in their lives.

Work Satisfaction depends on various factors. It is not always the salary or money you earn that attracts the person. Once, a young lady left her well-paying job in a reputed surveying institution to accept a less-paying job as a receptionist at a surgical hospital. Here, the salary and other facilities, terms and conditions were substandard; but she liked this job a lot. When she was questioned about it, she said happily and enthusiastically, "1) I like meeting people, and it is possible here. 2) I really feel that my work is an essential sacred act. 3) The troubled patients who come here thank me for my assistance to them. They express their gratitude and satisfaction. It gives me a great pleasure. 4) I have a special importance, esteem and respect here. 5) I have an authority to serve the people in suffering. So I am especially interested in this job. I have been working here since last five years. I was never late in these five years. I had an attractive salary and other nice facilities where I worked earlier, yet I never used to be on time to the work. I used to be bored while going to work there…" She told many such things. Several such examples can be found.

One of my friends graduated in Law with the first rank in the university. He won the Gold Medal. Many people advised him to practise law at the Supreme Court at Delhi. "You will wallow in wealth. You will eat from a silver spoon." They said to him. But, without falling prey to any of these temptations, he accepted the teaching profession which gave him comparatively less money. It was a conscious decision. In the four decades of his service, he guided and nurtured many generations of students. He enjoyed his profession, and with a satisfied mind, he retired from his job. He is still doing his favourite job of teaching, just out of passion. He works as an advisor for various NGOs.

Many experts and psychologists have noted their observations regarding Work and Work Culture, as well as liking and passion for work. Various research papers have been presented. All these documents sum up only one thing: "If an individual gets the work of his/her interest, he/she does it enthusiastically, wholeheartedly and speedily. He/she performs the work as spontaneously as if it is some interesting play. Such work constantly gives a positive energy to the person, and makes him/her forget all the worries and problems. He/she even does not care for material facilities. The individuals or groups who work in this way, become centers of happiness, satisfaction and create a paradise."

Summing up: If you want to achieve happiness, satisfaction, joy and expertise in the work throughout your life, experience the fun in doing the work of your interest and choice.

***

7. HAPPINESS, HEALTH AND WORK

Principle: A person's happiness depends on his health and his involvement in work.

Explanation: An expert named Friedrich Herzberg draws a conclusion in his book titled *Work and the Nature of Man*: "Our health and our happiness depend on our work." Every individual may have his/her own different view on Health, Happiness and Work. There are multiple such views. But, the person who continuously does the work of his interest leads a happy, contented and healthy life; because he gets a pure and real joy of 'self-actualisation' through work. A separate chapter in this book is dedicated to this thought.

It is, after all, for the well-being of a person that he/she should work. If a person does not get a meaningful and interesting work to, he/she becomes psychologically handicapped and physically sluggish. There are many farmers and farm labourers in my village who have meager income barely adequate to fulfill their basic needs. They constantly work in their field without paying heed to the blazing sun or torrential rain or chilling cold. They work in fresh air and free atmosphere. But I have seldom seen them suffering from diabetes, blood pressure, stomachache, headache or such ailments. They live a long and healthy life. Because they are always engaged in their work. They are fast asleep as soon as they lie on bed. They get up early, before sunrise. They do not need sleeping pills or a peg of drink for a peaceful sleep; nor do they need to set an alarm for getting up early.

However, nowadays, villages are shrinking fast and cities are bulging. It has been resulting in various health issues. Herzberg opines, "The most essential need of a human being is to attain his mental development as a creative individual through work as per his capabilities and according to the situation." He has illustrated through various incidents and persons that any human being can achieve his optimum development through work. Just as sight and hearing are different and relative for each individual, the nature of everyone's work can also be different from others. Mental development is the most prominent need of any individual, which can be fulfilled through meaningful, challenging and creative work. A person can be happy, contented and healthy in real sense only when he achieves this development.

Some stages in mental development:

1. **Enhancement of knowledge**: Every individual should enhance his/her knowledge to bring accuracy, perfection and quality to work. It is necessary to keep learning through experiences, mistakes as well as through success and failures. That is why it is rightly said that 'experience is the best teacher'.
2. **Interest**: If you are interested in the accepted work, this interest should be developed in an ascendance with the help of knowledge and experience. The person who works should feel that the work is as interesting as some pleasurable and inspiring play. It grooms the personality to be effective.
3. **Creativity**: It is important to implement new ideas and concepts in the accepted work, and to consciously get rid of outdated methods to bring relevance to the work. It is creativity that gives birth to innovation. It is the reason man could make such discoveries. It is the lack of creativity that prevents other animals, birds and creatures from inventing new things.
4. **Knowledge and Understanding**: It is possible that a person has theoretical knowledge of the work to do. But he may not necessarily have understood the work in minute details. For instance, a person can know the theory of writing poetry by heart, but it does not necessarily mean that he knows the deep

or implied meanings and imagery of the poem. The same is applicable to a theory. Therefore, it is expected that the person should have the knowledge and deep understanding of the work he is going to start.

5. **Ambiguity and uncertainty**: The work you are doing may have various ambiguities and uncertainties in it. The reasons can be varied. For instance, there was a huge ambiguity and uncertainty about Coronavirus disease in its initial days. No one had a hint that it would turn into such a horrible pandemic and spread across globe. Everyone was ignorant about the impending monstrous crisis and its probable impacts on various factors. A person's world can turn upside down due to many reasons – unannounced natural calamities like earthquakes, tsunami, tempests, torrential rains, wildfires, or calamities like accidents, illness... so on and so forth. They may even wipe out one's existence.

   Therefore, if a person is aware of these things while working, he can attain his holistic and complete development. In absence of this understanding, one may possibly get nothing but failure, defeat, or just a partial success. Hence, a person can attain meaning of his life only if he gets involved in the work he does. A thinker called Lorenz states about Work, "Doing work half-heartedly or lazily can give you a transient pleasure, but it cannot give a lasting happiness."

Montagu Norman (1871-1950) was the Governor of the Bank of England during 1920 to 1944. No other person has held this position for so long as him. When he was young, he had been suffering from severe headache and hallucinations. He was so depressed by his illness that he neither met nor talked to anyone. Around 1911, he faced severe psychological issues. He was bedridden for two months. He could remember nothing. For many elongated weeks, he had helplessly lied in his gloomy room, getting treatment for his unbearable headache. His doctors assumed that he will survive barely for a few months. Later, he was advised to consult Dr Roger Vittoes of Switzerland, an expert in such illnesses. Dr Roger advised Montagu Norman to "focus solely on the work. The work should be so nerve-racking that there should be no time to think of anything else." This advice proved miraculous in Montagu Norman's case. He attained peace of mind through it. Later he worked for twenty-four years as the Governor of the Bank of England, and became a highly accomplished man. He earned a great satisfaction and happiness through it.

Finally, as Herzberg says in his *Work and the Nature of Man*, "Our health and happiness depend on our work", many examples can prove this. Thus, it explains how delightful and healthy it is to accept and get engrossed in some work.

Summing up: A person's happiness, satisfaction and his financial earning depend on nothing but his work. Work can be an effective remedy for several psychological diseases.

***

8. WORK: SCOPE AND NEED

Principle: Work, its nature, scope and need can be largely varied.

Explanation: Every individual has some small or large professional circles. Some people may have very small professional circles whereas some others may have very expanded circles. The world of Work is very interesting and fascinating. This world seems to be arranged in an ascending order: the individual, family, society, village, city, state, nation, and ultimately the entire world. Here, we are concerned only about the work of human beings, and not about other animals. The humans' world of work is full of constant ups and downs, and often dissatisfaction and tumults. Yet, it is only the work that helps the person attain the eventual happiness and satisfaction. It may feel good to stay without work for a day or two, or even for a few weeks or months. We can call it rest or relaxation. During the Corona pandemic, it was all well in the initial few days, weeks or months. Later, it felt like being imprisoned in your own home, which was quite disturbing. That is why the ultimate goal of life is not to stay idle. On the contrary, if you maintain neatness, good quality and consistency in work, it would certainly lead you to the accomplishment of yourself, your family, and in turn everyone else around you. You can prove your abilities only through work. Of course, the person's approach towards work and the methods used for work matter a lot.

Maslow, the father of Humanitarian Psychology, has clearly said that "A person's development and progress depend on the standard and quality of his work. The person's work becomes an inseparable part of his personality." In short, a person's work holds a mirror to his personality. Looking at the person's work, you can guess about the person and even know the prospective direction of his/her progress.

A hardworking farmer purchased a piece of land with his hard earned money. When he grew old, he divided the land in two equal parts between his two sons. Both the sons started tilling their piece of land. But there was a huge difference in their methods, objectives and perspectives of working. Naturally, there was huge difference in their income, too. The elder son earned more income than the younger son. Both of them, in fact, had received the land of same size and quality. The climate, rainfall, water and other factors were exactly the same for both. Still their incomes largely differed from each other. What was the reason? I don't think it needs a detailed explanation.

Maslow, throughout his life, studied the mindsets and mental diseases of the working individuals. He has recorded his observations as follows: "It is not the complete truth that you can cure a person using psychiatry. Most of the people are constantly in search of happiness. But they do not necessarily find it. They can attain their desired happiness through their continuous and meaningful work." He says at last, "A person can attain salvation through doing his/her destined or assigned or necessary work, to the best of his capacity."

In brief, Work subtly nurtures an individual's personality, making it rich, effective and respectable. Work gives meaning to life. It gives ultimate happiness, satisfaction and joy. Activeness, promptness, conscience and objective behind work are the four factors that lay the foundation of an accomplished life. When a person passionately loves his accepted work, he can achieve the progress for himself and his family, as well as builds a high culture.

Work is a mere source of earning money for many people. However, the approaches towards work largely differ from person to person, regarding the nature and purpose of work. This is the reason why one individual gets happiness and satisfaction through work while another does not. One is spontaneous while another is a slacker. One regards work as sacred as worship while another as painful as a punishment. Thus the prism of Work diffracts varied colors and shades. Needs, feelings and mindsets differ from person to person, and they are fulfilled only through Work. Hence, it will be wrong to make a sweeping statement like 'every person works only for money, fame and prestige.'

Some people – an individual or a group of individuals, like labour unions –either stop working or work sluggishly, even if they are in need of work. There may be various reasons and purposes behind it. Sometimes there may be a noble cause or some good intention whereas sometimes it may be just a selfish cause. Hence, the angles of Work and work psychology are myriad and complex.

An ordinary worker in a steel factory at Durgapur was assigned the task of bringing crowbar. Once, his senior officer asked him to bring the crowbar. He refused, and this apparently simple incident culminated in a huge strike in the factory. In 1926, there was a big strike in England. Press workers in the printing press of Daily Mail refused to print an editorial titled 'For the King and the Nation', as they felt it provocative. In 1972, workers in the factory of General Motors announced a strike. What they demanded was not a raise in wages, but a meaningful work. They demanded a high quality work-life. Thus, it is difficult to accurately judge a work-related situation. Even petty reasons such as someone's hurt ego can also lead to strikes.

Today, the spectrum of work is rapidly changing due to numerous reasons such as growing facilities of education, technological advancements, people's needs, vastness and variety in marketplaces, changing lifestyle with its pros and cons, rapid availability of transport and communication, and so on. No matter whether we like it or not, we have to accept this reality, because it will accordingly change the nature of work.

Summing up: Scope, objectives, nature, place and time of work may change according to changing needs, but work is the only remedy on many complex issues.

***

9. WORK: MIRROR TO THE PERSONALITY

Principle: Work is the best mirror for an individual's personality.

Explanation: Work holds a mirror to an individual's personality. The person can behold his true self in the work only. When a person works with a full vigor and enthusiasm, we can know with certainty the person is perfectly fine, both physically and mentally. Only a person who is physically and mentally fit and fine can do his/her work with maintaining a high quality. Work speaks about a person and personality. It reveals how a person and his/her work are closely connected. Work speaks about the background, education, upbringing, motivations, values and cultural background of a person. Hence, our work is an objective scale to measure our progress and development. Now, everyone knows the difference between industrious and lazy persons on the parameters like their symptoms, behavior and thoughts.

Two sons of the same father inherited equal areas of equally fertile land. One of them works carefully, devotedly and punctually, while another is lazy and insincere. As a result, there is a vast difference in the incomes both of them get from the land. It casts a huge impact on their personalities and lives. The diligent son lives a more enthusiastic, optimistic and happy life, whereas the insincere one gets a meager income and leads a miserable life, cursing his fate. We might have heard or read about many such examples. 'A mirror will show your reflection as you are.' A mirror never lies. Work is no exception, either. Therefore, work speaks.

Despite getting similar facilities and amenities, the outcomes of the work may be different, because different individuals have different tendencies and different extents of virtues and vices. Once, Dhirubhai Ambani, a renowned businessman, was travelling to attend an important meeting in which many other businessmen were participating. But alas! Suddenly the weather changed and there was a stormy rainfall and tempestuous winds. Most of the people parked their cars beside the road and waited for the storm to subside. Seeing them, Dhirubhai's driver suggested stopping the car. But Dhirubhai did not allow him to stop. He asked him to keep going carefully and a bit slowly. When they travelled 8-10 kilometres more, they reached where there was no rain and the weather was sunny and cheerful. Dhirubhai thus reached the venue of the meeting on time. Those who kept waiting, could not. Obviously, it was Dhirubhai who got the big contract of the work. Dhirubhai Ambani's perseverance and his courage to overcome obstacles were some of the secret keys to the rapid growth of his company. These sensibilities, capacities, persistence, perseverance and courage are highly significant among the various attributes of personality development.

Everyone has a desire to do some or other work. Human body is a living organism. It needs air, water and food to generate the energy required to work. In other words, this energy gets converted into behaviour. 'Work' is a part of that behavior. 'Work' is an outlet for the physical and mental energy that is constantly being generated in a human body. Absolute lack of work suffocated a person. A famous author has said, "You ask me why I work. The answer is quite simple. I work for the same reason why a hen lays eggs. My work holds a mirror to me. Work is a thing of pleasure for me. Work not only sustains but enhances my enthusiasm. Who am I? How am I? What kind of personality do I have? … If you want to know these and such things, look at my work. Do a fair evaluation, and you will understand everything about me."

Summing up: The relation between a person, his personality and his work is like a chain. Each part of this chain is linked with the other.

***

10. WORK: THE BEST TEACHER

Principle: *Guru* (teacher) is the one who gives right direction to your life; the one who guides you. Work does precisely the same.

Explanation: There are many things in life, which cannot be taught. They can only be learnt. A baby fish does not need someone to teach it how to swim. It learns swimming naturally. It is a well-known saying that 'experience makes man perfect'. A great singer never misses his daily *riyaz* (practice), because only this *riyaz* enhances his expertise.

In rural areas and remote settlements, many people are illiterate. Yet, they can easily predict the weather conditions by reading natural phenomena like birds' nests, their behaviour etc. At times, their predictions prove even more accurate than a climatologist's. There was a stone-cutter named Shankar Dhotre in our village. He initially worked as a labourer. Later, he became a construction contractor, powered by his long work experience, observation skills, and tendency to work hard. He was completely uneducated, as far as formal education is concerned. He was illiterate. Yet, he could accurately tell how deep a pit is, how many brass of sand could be extracted from it, how much stone or sand is required for a particular construction, and so on. Who taught him all this? Which school did he go to learn all this? The answer is: he achieved all this due to his constant practice and long experience of work. Once, he gave the accurate estimate of the sand that could be extracted from a pit. When his subordinate, who was an engineer, actually measured the sand, it was precisely what Shankar had estimated. When they asked him about his precise judgement, he answered, "Work itself is my *guru*. No one taught me anything. I made mistakes while working. I realised my mistakes, and improved on them. I kept working with dedication and perseverance." Dhotre's words of experience prove that 'Work is the best teacher.' Education also means learning from experience and work.

There is another such example that I have seen: my grandmother. She was the head of our large joint family of 30-35 people. Four sons, three daughters, daughters in-law, grandchildren—all lived together in the house. All the food required for so many people was cooked under her supervision and guidance. But there was never a single error in cooking so much food for so many people—not a pinch of salt more or less; not a spoon of sugar more or less; no fuss at home despite so many people living together. This accuracy was my grandmother's routine for so many years. Despite being an illiterate woman, and without doing any course in management, my grandmother had achieved this accuracy throughout her life.

Once, all of us had gathered in our village home for Diwali celebrations. My grandmother had prepared tasty delicacies for all of us. While relishing them, I asked her, "Granny, how can you do all this so smoothly? Who taught it to you? Who is your teacher?" She answered very frankly, "There is no *guru* or teacher, my child. I was my own teacher. I kept learning through work. Work itself is my teacher." We all, so called 'educated' grandchildren, were astonished to hear her answer. There are many such 'self-made' students in these villages and remote settlements. Of course, it cannot be achieved in a day or a week or a month. Years of dedicated and sincere hardwork lead to such accomplishments.

Galbraith is famous for his book titled *The New Industrial State*, which is considered as a fundamental discourse in the industrial sector. However, this book did not materialise easily within just a year or two. Galbraith had been working on it for ten years. He drafted this discourse three or four times, yet he was not satisfied with it. He started writing this book in 1957. He used to draft it, cross it, and redraft it. Finally, after four years, i.e. in 1961, he could prepare the elementary draft. Meanwhile he was appointed as the Ambassador in India. Therefore, he kept the manuscript in a vault in the bank. After his tenure in India ended, he returned and started re-thinking on his topic with a new perspective. He discarded the earlier draft in which he had invested four long years of hard work. Galbraith thus concluded that 'every author should take a long vacation before publishing the discourse so that he could contemplate over it and rewrite it. Such revision gives perfection to the work. Eventually, it becomes our teacher and guide.'

There are many classic works of literature in various languages: Ian Hamilton's (1853-1947) *Soul of the Army*, Maxim Gorkey's *The Mother*, Ranajit Desai's *Swami*, Shivaji Sawant's *Mrityunjay*, Bhalchandra Nemade's Kosla, and so on. These authors worked really hard to create these great pieces of literature. Their hard work made these texts the immortal works of literature. The summary of what these writers say is: "There should be a focus on accuracy right from the beginning. You cannot fly very high on the wings of imagination. An understanding, consciousness and experience of reality are required for it." E.g. Imagine, you walk on a wooden plank kept on the carpet in your living room, and also imagine another situation when you walk on a wooden plank kept hanging on a 500 feet deep vale – they are completely different experiences. It is easy to suggest simple solutions for complex problems in a seminar, with the help of very nice presentations. But in reality, sometimes you cannot solve even simple problems in life. A skilled professor of Economics may fail to do even simple calculations, but an illiterate street vendor can easily do the same.

In brief, the experience of actual work is the best teacher. This teacher is kind, as well as strict. It teaches a lot without uttering a single word. It enlightens us, guides us and helps us. It continuously watches us, and tests our likes, dislikes, efficiency, loyalty and perseverance. We have to respect this teacher called Work. We have to strive for perfection while respecting it.

Summing up: Formal education is undoubtedly important. However, actual experience of work can teach a lot. Hence, work is the true teacher.

***

11. INVOLVEMENT IN WORK

Principle: Involvement in Work means using the best and the all of our capacity while working.

Explanation: Why do people work? When can they work at their best? Many experts and researchers in India and abroad have tried to find answers to these questions. They reached some conclusions which are certainly useful for those who wish to work – especially for a group of workers who work as a team. 1) Productivity of the work done by workers depends simply on the salary they get. 2) The team spirit like 'this is our work and we are doing it for our sake' is seen. 3) Workers have an urge for the usefulness, recognition and honour of their work. 4) Collective work is done not merely for getting petty concessions, but out of a noble and inclusive feeling among the workers. 5) They wish they should have importance at the workplace. A worker's involvement in the workplace management gives an inner satisfaction, since it enhances their commitment to productivity. This is the reason why a respectful harmony is expected between the owner and the workers.

Prof. Elten Mayo was a noble-hearted and enthusiastic researcher. He conducted a valuable research in the complex field of human relations in industries. The above mentioned points are the conclusions of his research. During 1927 to 1932, he conducted an extensive research at a factory at Hawthorn near Chicago, U.S., where around 30,000 workers were employed.

This factory always used to have a heated atmosphere. They conducted an experiment here, called 'the first relay assembly test room'. Productivity of a group of five girls who manufactured a part of telephone was studied. In the first stage of this experiment, multiple variants were examined to see which of them influences the productivity of this group. For this, various changes were made. More time was allowed to have a break from work. A system of lumpsum payment was introduced. The policy of five-day week was implemented. But in the last stage of this experiment, a dramatic change was made: all the concessions given to the group were withdrawn.

Surprisingly, the girls did not oppose or rebel against this, as it was expected. On the contrary, there was a growth in their productivity. In fact they set a new record of production. Thus, Elton Mayo concluded that it is a grave misconception that productivity depends on money. Work is a collective activity, and a feeling of inclusiveness/ involvement matters a lot. It is important for a person that his work is recognised, his work proves useful, and his inner feelings are satiated through the respect he wins for his work.

An in-depth study of the psychology of teams always supports the fact that teamwork leads to good quality, standard and productivity. A widow in a village started a small scale domestic business of preparing pickles and other home-made food products. Nowadays, since working women have no time to cook these items at home, they prefer such readymade products. The widow understood the market need, and she started the business by forming more such small groups of rural women who were merely housewives by then. She divided these teams in yet smaller groups and distributed tasks amongst them. As the business grew, she hired some more women. When the business achieved better growth, she founded a company named Annapurna Udyog. Today, around 150 self-help groups are working for Annapurna Udyog. They are managing the business collectively as owners. They invest a part of their income in the business, and they get good returns as well. Thus they are committed and involved in their business. They are not just workers but owners of their business. It is the commitment and involvement towards their work that has earned them a good reputation.

Summing up: A worker's involvement in production as an owner, leads to the high quality and quantity of the product.

***

12. DILIGENCE IN WORK

Principle: Diligence, or industrious nature, in work is beneficial and inspiring for all.

Explanation: Economists say, 'Human resource is the wealth of nation.' However, this statement needs to be viewed from a perspective of consistent, qualitative and hardworking tendency and intense patriotism. The power, capabilities, expertise, intellect, creativity and knowledge of the human resource should be used for the worthwhile production or service. All other non-living resources in the nation cannot produce anything on their own. Only human resource can utilise all other resources for innovation. Only human beings can invent new machines and technologies. Only human beings can use their work and imagination for innovation. In brief, Work performed by a human being is the soul of all change, development and transformation. It has been proven again and again. The Work here includes all types of individual and collective activities.

An individual, a society and a nation—all need each other's works. A famous author George Bernard Shaw says, "A nation needs thinkers, teachers, workers, and it also has an equal – rather more – need of sweepers. If they don't do their work, would thinkers, writers, teachers and poets clean the garbage collected every day? If the answer is in negative, then everyone's work is equally important, respectable and worthy of honour." Therefore, no work is ever negligible, avoidable or unimportant. It is the collective spirit in small and trivial works that leads to the success of grand projects. Many trivial things often lead to revolutionary changes. It is a sign of gentility and sophistication to respect and honour everyone's work, without looking down upon it.

It is the housewives' work that helps men to do their jobs outside smoothly. Tiny ants can build a huge anthill. Small creatures like earth worms can disintegrate even rocks to create fertile soil for crops and trees to grow—all these environment-friendly works are continuously done by tiny creatures like ants, earthworms, insects, birds and so on. They help the cycle of nature run smoothly. We can understand how important everyone's work is, just by having a glance at these examples.

The culture and efficiency of a factory or industry depends on the workers who work there and the well-organised management. When each worker performs his/her task devotedly, the factory or the industry can achieve transformation rapidly. This formula of work is also applicable to an individual, a family, society and even nation. Eventually, it is the faith in, passion for and consistency in work that leadsa nation, a family and an individual to its progress and upliftment.

Diligence or industrious nature is the wealth of an individual, a family, a society and a nation. If all other resources are available but diligence is absent, the other resources become worthless. It is all right even if the resources are absent or deficient, but absence of diligence is never all right. If one is diligent, he can grow greenery on the barest of rocks. But if the person is not diligent, even a fertile land would be useless for him. It highlights the importance of diligence in work.

Dedication and involvement in work is more important than egoism. It is sheer nonsense to assume that only 'I' do everything. Although it is a fact that some works depend on the individual's own skills, it is ultimately the diligence of everyone involved in the work that helps lead a fulfilled and quality life. "An army fights bravely on the battlefield, but there are thousands and lakhs of people who perform their work diligently and give them an indirect support." It is very important to understand and internalise the meaning of this statement. It is equally important to develop an all-inclusive perspective towards diligence while working. It will materialise the progress of an individual, a family, a society and the nation.

Summing up: Work, and diligence in working, is essential for holistic development. 'Unity is strength' is the *mantra* of diligence in work.

***

13. MORAL RESPONSIBILITY IN WORK

Principle: Moral involvement and commitment is important for work.

Explanation: We can live alone. We can even achieve progress and earn name and fame alone. However, we often forget that it all depends, directly or indirectly, on the work of thousands of people. Such ungrateful forgetting dries the fountainhead of pure joy in our life. We need many things to live comfortably, right from when we get up till, we go to bed. Can we – and do we – create all these things on our own? Let's take an example of tea, coffee or milk that we have every morning. Are they produced through our work? Do we produce the stove, matchbox, cups, saucers, filters and so on? No. Hundreds of people keep working to produce them. It is only then that we can have our tea or coffee. Feel gratitude for the person responsible for, or working for, producing your objects of pleasure; and the consumption of those objects will give you a unique delight. This gratitude is nothing but the morality in work. Every member of a family performs his/ her share of work. That's why a family can function in a well-organised way. In brief, there are many invisible hands that support our existence and comfort. It is our moral responsibility to always be grateful to them. Etiquette of saying 'thank you' is rooted in this very feeling.

Everyone can create only a few products or provide a few services; but everyone requires a number of other products and services, and wants them to be of good quality. However, if we fail to perform our work well, or cannot maintain good quality, we have no moral right to expect high quality products or services from others.

I got to read an interesting incident during the Corona pandemic. Some young nurses were travelling in a bus. The bus conductor was a rude man and hence there was a war of words between him and the nurses. At the same time, the bus met with a severe accident. The conductor was injured and was taken to the same hospital where the nurses were working. The conductor was treated very badly in the hospital. The Union of Transport Workers raised voice against the nurses. But, if we think with a balanced mind, the conductor who treats his passengers rudely cannot have a right to receive courteous treatment from others. That's why it is rightly said, 'As you sow, so shall you reap.' The same principle as mentioned in the *Bhagavad Gita* is also applicable to the morality in work.

E.F. Schumacher states about the moral responsibility in work, in his contemplative book titled *Small is Beautiful*: "Educated people owe a great deal to the society. For any student who takes primary, secondary and higher education, it is the farmers, workers, and other professionals in the society who have to spend their money. They have to work for earning that money. Therefore, every educated person should be aware of his indebtedness to various social sectors. Hence, it is a moral responsibility of every individual to do some or other contribution to the society." He further says, "Is education a license to earn profit for ourselves or a sacred bond of service to people?" Everyone has to think over this question while acquiring and giving education. If we consider involvement and commitment as the soul of education – and if we act upon this thought – life will be easier and happier. Therefore, the doctors, engineers, teachers, professors—everyone who gets educated through the society's money paid in the form of tax, must do something to repay this debt. Nowadays, we find a growing number of the educated people who live self-centred and materialistic life and detach themselves from social service. What kind of downfall is this? A tendency to think for the 'me' and 'my family', and to avoid the moral responsibility in work, is bound to lead us to a certain downfall.

In the world history, there were many educated young men and women who sacrificed their personal comfort and luxuries for social service. They devoted themselves to serving society in various fields. Bharat Ratna Ishwar Chandra Vidyasagar, Nanaji Deshmukh, Baba Amte, Jayprakash Narayan, Acharya Vinoba Bhave… the list goes very long. Just like in our country, there have been such great personages in other countries as well. Now it is time to think whether the dwindling number of such personalities is a sign of progression or regression.

World has a long and glorious tradition of such noble personalities and their contribution. Their only goal was to uplift the society and they worked to realise this goal. Many people in political, academic, scientific, agricultural, professional and industrial sectors have done enormous work which stands tall like a lighthouse. They used to regard social service above all. Social service was a great morality for them. They immersed themselves working in their chosen fields, and attained the joy of 'self-actualisation' through it. Education is not confined to acquiring sheer bookish knowledge, getting a stable life, living a life full of materialistic pleasures with an ungrateful outlook towards society, and frantically leading a virtual life.

Downfall of morality in various walks of life can lead to dark prospects of the individual, his/her family, society and in turn the whole country. Pure happiness lies in working with a high preference to morality, no matter what kind of the work is. (A special section in this book is dedicated to the Work Ethics.)

Summing up: Lack of morality in working or getting work done eventually leads to everyone's downfall.

***

14. WORK: MOTIVATIONS AND FLAWS

Principle: Motivation is and should be at the root of every work. As you realise flaws and errors in work, you should be motivated to remove them.

Explanation: If Work is inspired by a comprehensive motivation and if its execution is flawless, it is possible to attain well-being and development of oneself as well as others. In this regard, the Constitution of India states, "Everyone should always attempt to bring perfection in work, in all individual and collective sectors. It will help our nation to achieve new heights of success in its activities and initiatives." D.C. McClelland, a great psychologist, analyses the phenomenon of economic development in his classic discourse titled *The Achieving Society*. Though his presented in the light of his times, it is equally relevant in present age as well. In his opinion, there is a particular human desire that is mainly responsible for economic development. He called this desire as 'Need for Achievement' (nAch). He researched a lot even in India. According to him, Indians lag behind in 'Need for Achievement' and hence their economic development is not speedy. Therefore, motivational thoughts, motivating individuals and means to provide work motivation are important.

Inspiring individuals show some distinct characteristics: 1) They prefer perfection in work over money, honour and power. 2) While accepting any work, they preferentially think about the scope for excellence rather than financial benefit or recognition. 3) They are always ready to work with others. 4) They prefer the experts and hardworking people as their work partners over their friends, relatives or acquaintances. 5) They prefer to be successful by doing something innovative rather than accumulating wealth by any other means. 6) They focus on achieving success rather than evading failures. 7) They give a deep and multifarious thought to the pros and cons/ merits and demerits/ profit and loss in various schemes of work. 8) They are very cautious about the present and prospective need of various schemes. 9) They are visionary, realistic and interested in long-term planning. 10) They independently think on the roadmap of work on the basis of their experiences and values. They seek help of other, too, if necessary. 11) They can quickly judge the changing scenario and think over it practically. 12) They instinctively seek relevant solutions on the sudden unforeseen problems. 13) They are insistent upon the meticulous planning, and preparing the blueprint of the work before actually starting it. 14) They never compromise with their values to complete the work anyhow.

Considering the importance of nAch – Need for Achievement, McClelland says in his *The Achieving Society*, "Experts in the child development should be sent to the developing countries. They should guide parents in these countries about how to develop Need for Achievement among their children."

'Need for Achievement' is characterised by an ambition to bring relevant improvements in the work, and especially an efficient handling of financial aspects. It is the desire to bring perfection to work – nota mundane desire to earn sheer profit out of it – that leads to the subsequent economic development. A person is ultimately evaluated on the basis of motivation that drives him/her to workwith consistency and persistence. It is a reality that money is essential to fulfil needs and wants. Also, money is earned through work. Yet, it is only meticulous and planned hardwork, self-discipline, simple lifestyle and an urge to achieve a concrete goal that form the roots of nAch (Need for Achievement).

Although various measures are taken to nurture motivation for work, but they do not always prove fruitful. For instance, the scheme was aimed at improving the standard of life of the fishermen in Kakinada, Andhra Pradesh. These fishermen used to do fishing and earn very meagre income that was barely adequate to fulfil their basic needs. Their fishing nets were fragile. On noticing this, the Government arranged for them strong nylon nets of considerably bigger size which could contain more fish. It was expected that the fishermen would get more catch, andin turn more income, due to these nets. More the income, more would have been the savings. Ultimately it would have led to the utilisation of money for some good cause. This was the noble design behind the scheme.

The reality was exactly opposite. Some of the fishermen used to stop work after getting their regular catch. Those who got more catch and more income, spent their money inaddictions and in enjoying various cheap luxuries. This is how the nice schemes meet their tragic end, and the Need for Achievement goes in vain. A sophisticated farmer of my acquaintance built toilets for the tribal farm labourers on his farm. My farmer friend had thought that it would save time and increase hygiene of the labourers, and consequently they would work better to produce better yield in turn. He had intended to arouse the nAch (Need for Achievement) among them. He always used to tell us how he was taking efforts for their betterment. We were impressed by his good deed. But alas! He told us just after a few days, "Those toilets proved useless. My labourers store wood there and go in the open space to respond the calls of nature." We were dumbfounded to hear this. This is the reason why some psychologists have noted that "a useful act can turn into a useless one, if a drive for self-development is absent in those for whomthe it is done."

The American Friends Service Committee implemented a *Gramseva Yojana* (Village Service Scheme) at a village in Odisha during 1952 to 1962. They invested a capital of Rs. 60 lakhs (in those days) in this scheme. Objectives of this scheme were as follows: 1) People should get pure drinking water. 2) They should use toilets to prevent diseases/ epidemics. 3) They should plant vegetables and do poultry farming. 4) They should form a cooperative society each for leather workers and weavers. Villagers were made involved in this scheme. They were counselled from time to time,to understand their needs, desires and aspirations. After ten years, Dr. Thomas Fraser, a researcher in the field of humanities, drew following conclusions from the outcomes of this scheme: 1) This scheme availed 154 wells along with water pumps on them. These wells provided the villagers with pure drinking water. 2) Initially, the villagers produced more vegetables owing to the availability of water, but since there was no provision for their sale, the prices fell, and villagers gave up the practice of growing vegetables. 3) They started keeping foreign breeds of hens instead of indigenous breeds. The foreign breeds need more care and protection which was absent there, and therefore dogs easily preyed on these chickens. As a result, the indigenous breed of chickens was also destroyed in an attempt to bring improvements. The scheme proved utterly fruitless because the beneficiaries themselves lacked the Need for Achievement. The cooperative societies were doing well in the initial phase. However, later, the work was brought down to ground zero due to the disputes and rivalry amongst the concerned members. According to Fraser and McClelland, many such schemes failed owing to the absence of nAch (Need for Achievement) in the beneficiaries.

'Need for Achievement' can be awakened through appropriate educational activities. D.C. McClelland mentions in his classic discourse *The Achieving Society* certain human motivations that are responsible for economic development and progress. Therefore, various educational activities should be implemented from time to time to awaken the Need for

Achievement in employees so that they would work more effectively. For this, it is necessary to execute innovative and relevant activities and take a timely review of them. Several reputed companies across the world are actively careful about awakening the Need for Achievement among their employees. Naturally, such companies, organisations and individuals can easily survive in the world full of competition.

Hence, every individual should keep improving upon his work in order to make it perfect and excellent. Need for Achievement is essential to achieve progress in every field, and to cope up with the growing competition. Only if you keep a weapon always polished, it can be of use in the battle. The same rule is applicable to the Need for Achievement in work. A sense of perfection is highly beneficial in every work. It can save a person from depression. It can create a sublime work culture of diligence. An amendment in the Constitution of India says, "Everyone should strive to bring perfection in all individual and public sectors. It is what will help the nation to ascend the path of success."

Summing up: The supreme inspiration or nAch (Need for Achievement) bring excellence to the work. But lack of nAch leads to nothing; it just wastes energies of the person and is absolutely fruitless.

***

15. INDUSTRY AND ECONOMY IN WORK

Principle: Industry and economy are the expected qualities in the execution of any work.

Explanation: Madhav Patil of my village is a remarkable and inspiring example of industry and economy in work. Although not very educated, Madhav Patil heads a large joint family of four sons, three daughters and five brothers. All the five brothers, with their wives and children, live together even in today's era of nuclear family. I always wonder which bond has kept them together.

Madhav Patil and his brothers started as farm laborers. They had no other option since they held only a small piece of land and lived below poverty line. Despite their hardships, they were very diligent, sincere and punctual. They used to every work with personal affinity towards it; it was their core value. Naturally, they had earned a great respect not only in their village but also in neighbouring villages.

Madhav Patil made a remarkable progress on account of his inherent qualities. Within a few years, he owned a farm with the help of his industry (habit of working hard) and economy (habit of spending money very carefully). The then Mahadu or Madhav had now become 'Madhavrao Patil, a successful industrious farmer'. As they say, Rome was not built in a day. The progress of Madhavrao's family was no exception to this saying. He, along with his family members, toiled hard for a whole decade. He spent his earnings frugally, and used the saved money to buy agricultural lands. Now he is a progressive and skilled landlord. He tilled his lands by working there in a planned and systematic way. All the five brothers have their own bungalows in close proximity. These bungalows are named as 'Meethbhakar No. 1', 'Meethbhakar No. 2', 'Meethbhakar No. 3', 'Meethbhakar No. 4' and 'Meethbhakar No. 5'. The marathi word 'meetbhakar' means salt and roti, which is the food of poorest of poors. The construction of and the facilities in all the five bungalows are exactly similar to each other. We read stories of *Pandavas* – the five brothers in the Mahabharata, but Madhavrao Patil's family is no less united than *Pandavas*. They have become an ideal family for all in the vicinity, and it is because of their work culture and style.

Here is an interview of Madhavrao Patil published in a reputed magazine which would be surprising even for an economist.

Q: What is the secret of your prosperity?

MadhavPatil: Industry, hardwork. Saving the money by spending it economically. A habit of living and working together, and our being teetotalers.

Q: How far have you and your brothers been educated?

Madhav Patil: Not much. I haven't passed my matriculation. My brothers have barely completed their graduation.

Q: How did you develop the quality of working hard?

Madhav Patil: We grew up in rural area. We had many examples of hardwork everywhere around us: tiny ants who build a huge anthill by collecting small particles of soil, birds who build beautiful nests by collecting tiny grass-sticks with their tiny beaks, earthworms that create such a great fertilizer by collecting soil, and many more. We had these living examples before us. If these small creatures can accomplish such big tasks, why can't we human beings do it? We, too, can do something unique to bring transformation and make progress.

Q: Is there any connection between your and your brothers' hard work in the field, and your progress? Could you please explain in detail?

Madhav Patil: (Happily) Sure. A single grain sown in the soil gives a huge yield. Each plant of the crop has so many ears. Each ear has in turn multiple grains. It's really a miracle of nature that a single grain can produce thousands of ears and grains. Our family is quite like a homogenous ear of grains. What you sow so shall you reap. Your actions emerge from your thoughts and behavior. We went on working hard, we went on saving money. We learnt all this from the nature itself. We earned money from our field and we spent it on developing and enrichingthe same field.

Q: Do you want to suggest that only a careful investment of your savings gives you good returns?

Madhav Patil: Whatever you may say, but the formula of prosperity is: spend the money for the growth and prosperity of its source; earn more money from it, and enhance its productivity and quality. This is the formula of our industry, economy and growth.

I remembered the lecture of our Economics professor. Listening to Madhavrao Patil's thoughts on hardwork and economy, I became nostalgic and recalled my enchanted college days. I remembered various theories of economics that were taught to me in college. A.K. Dasgupta, a renowned economist, has stated, "Industry and economy are very essential qualities for growth in productivity. Many developed countries like Japan and other countries doubled and tripled their production. Most of them saved almost forty per cent of their gross domestic product and invested it in the quality enhancement of industries and business.

They did micro-planning and implementation of work." Attitude, objective and implementation are certainly supportive to growth.

Late V.M. Dandekar, a great economist, has stated a few things essential for achieving diligence in work. A few points in a lecture he had delivered in a Youth Festival are briefly stated further:

1. **Time**: Everyone in the world gets equal amount of time. Suppose, my friends, every morning, 24 hours arecreditedto our account. No matter whether we spend them or not, the balance of time in our account becomes 'zero' by the end of the day. Hence, a lot depends on how one uses the 24 hours he/she gets. Next morning, 24 hours are again credited to our account. 'Time' always keeps flowing. It stops for no one, neither for the rich nor for the poor. Understanding this universal truth, we should do a meticulous time management. That's why you should complete your scheduled work before time. Complete it at the scheduled moment. Be fullyfocussed while you work. Be fully carefree while you take rest. Ask yourself time and again, "Do I complete my work carefully and on time as per schedule? Is there a qualitative diligence? Do I get happiness from the work?" Your capacity of working will certainly enhance through such self-talk and self-questioning.

2. **Method**: Micro-planning of a work is highly essential before you start. Success of a work depends upon the method and execution of the work. Half of the success depends on it. Rest of the accomplishment follows the actual execution of work. That's why it is said that you win half of the battle just bysystematic planning.

3. **Energy/ potential**: A person should use the 100% of his own capacity/potential/energy and that of his colleagues. This is what is called achieving success by giving one's best.

4. **Attitude/perspective**: Work should be considered as a noble duty, with a sacred and dedicated attitude towards it. When we expect quality and excellence in work from others, we also must have the same feeling while working for others.
5. **Other**: You should reach the peak of quality and excellence by utilizing your knowledge, intellect, skills and time. Industry, economy and intense sincerity should be prioritized.

A few selected remarks on work: Progress of an individual, a family, an organization and eventually a nation, depends only on industry in work. 1) Pandit Nehru had once said in irritation, "We all are lazy and careless. Especially we do not make sufficient use of our organs, mind and brain for work. We also tend to skip intellectual hard work." 2) Lenin had said shortly after the Russian Revolution, "Soviet Russia should teach its people to work and only work continuously." 3) Renowned economist A.K. Dasgupta had said, "Diligence and economy are very essential for growth in productivity." 4) Gunnar Myrdal, winner of Nobel Prize for Economics, had said, "As far as the present situation of India is concerned, the first essential thing this country needs for rapid and remarkable development is that they should increase the productivity of workers. The success of economic planning in India depends on its human resource. Can India encourage its people to work more and better to increase productivity?"

Summing up: Work increases productivity. Productivity improves economic conditions. However, industry and economy (providence) are necessary for it.

***

16. CREATIVITY IN WORK

Principle: A tendency to do something different, something innovative that is beneficial and useful to all nurtures creativity.

Explanation: It is difficult and complicated to give a precise definition of an individual's creativity. 'Creativity' is possible in every walk of life and every field of work. Even a layman, worker, farmer, labourer, housewife, writer, poet, thinker—anyone can be creative. When a person – may it be a man, a woman, or a young boy or girl – creates something useful or beautiful, it is a blissful, ecstatic situation for the person. This tendency, mindset and thought in work is called creativity. When Archimedes made a discovery, he was so elated that he emerged naked out of his bathroom, and started running on the streets, shouting 'Eureka, Eureka!' Many such stories are told in case of renowned people in various fields. This is creativity in work.

There is no novelty or uniqueness in the routine work. But there can be a tendency to be on an endless quest for innovation and uniqueness. Farmers all over India and world have succeeded in inventing high-yielding efficient varieties of crops. E.g. An illiterate American farmer named George Rig could invent hybrid crops only because of his creativity. He focused on getting better yield in less time. He invented 120 varieties of hybrid crops. Today, these hybrid crops are used across world.

No matter what field you work in, it is an individual's creativity that adds innovation, beauty and neatness to the work. A creative person uses all his senses and capabilities of body and brain with optimum efficiency. Creativity depends upon various factors such as knowledge, experience, flexibility, confidence, intuition, and readiness to work hard consistently and relentlessly. It is rightly said that 'the tree of creativity is firmly rooted in the soil of relentless hardwork.' Thomas Alva Edison was possessed with a creative passion. The laboratory which he had built with great efforts was burnt to ashes in front of his eyes. Some of his colleagues deserted him. Even then, he did not let it affect his creativity. He said to his remaining colleagues who had stayed firmly with him, "Today all my mistakes have burnt to ashes. Let's start work afresh." Within next 21 days, he invented gramophone. This is a phenomenal example of creativity at its best. Development and transformation that is useful for all is rooted in the adaptability and perseverance.

Creativity cannot be 'standardized'. Different individuals can express their creativity in many different ways. Creativity in work is developed through a constant passion for work, or through being possessed by work. Mother Teresa earned universal recognition for her selfless service to Indian society. Once, she saw a dying woman in front of a reputed hospital in Calcutta. She tried hard to get the woman admitted to the hospital, but her efforts went in vain. Her creative instinct for social service was kindled by this incident. It is then that Mother Teresa decided to establish an organization for the dying and the destitute. This organization was called *Nirmal Hriday*. A similar incident happened with Baba Amte who devoted his life in the service to leprosy afflicted people. Saint Gadage Baba devoted his life to serve people, after he saw the extent of ignorance and superstitions in the society. Ill treatment received by Negroes at the hands of White people turned Barrister Mohandas Karamchand Gandi into Mahatma Gandhi. He found his aim in life. He discovered weapons like *Satyagraha*, non-violence, strikes, *morcha*s in order to fight against injustice. Various such examples of creativity are found in various fields. These people set new standards of excellence. A creative work no longer remains ordinary. It reaches new heights of fame and reputation. We can name various personages across various fields as the examples of creativity:

Karmaveer Bhaurao Patil, Rabindranath Tagore are some of these names.

Creativity should never get rusted. Creativity is required in every work, however trivial or important it may be. Creativity enhances the quality of work. Better production and new ways of selling the products can be discovered. An individual, family, organisations, factories and in turn the nation gains prosperity through the management of production and sale. Consistency, dedication, healthy attitude, support of the universal principles of *Satyam-Shivam-Sundaram* (Truth-Good-Beauty), and an ever-growing creativity to accompany all these qualities can certainly bestow happiness, satisfaction and prosperity.

Summing up: Creativity is like Oxygen for work. The better its level of saturation, the better quality of the work will be.

***

17. WORK: AN INTERESTING PLAY

Principle: You should feel the same joy while working which you feel while playing your favourite game.

Explanation: 'When a person regards his/her work like some favourite play, when he/she likes it, the person works using the best of his/her capacities, with loyalty, passion and forgetting oneself.' All of us know this psychology of work. That is why we see those people achieving success who devote themselves to the work of their interest. Wise parents, therefore, bestow freedom upon their children to choose the career of their own interest. Later, these children become successful in the field they choose. On the contrary, if parents impose on their children a stream of education they do not like, they possibly become unsuccessful. They consider it as a burden, instead of an interesting play. They keep doing their work only because it has to be done, against their wish.

We are three brothers. One of us had no interest in formal education, whereas our father wanted him to get higher education, and become well-settled and reputed. He provided our brother with all the facilities. He had arranged for him special tutors. However, he felt studies and education absolutely uninteresting. He could not focus on studies. Consequently, despite having all the facilities available, he could make a score barely sufficient to pass the matriculation exam. Our father was highly disappointed. He focused his aspirations on the other son, and provided him with all the facilities, but he proved himself even superior to the elder brother. In spite of a lot of efforts, he could not pass his tenth. The reason was: they considered education as some burdensome yoke.

However, my elder brother was passionate about agricultural experiments. My father was a farmer who tilled his land using conventional methods. My brother totally deviated from our father's traditional method of farming. Investing his innovation, hardwork and dedication, he simply transformed our farm. While working in the farm, he would be completely engrossed in his work like a hermit sitting in meditation. He would be engaged in his work like a skilled player is engrossed in his game. With the help of a few labourers, he brought revolutionary changes in our farm. He started using seeds that give returns in less time, new methods like drip irrigation and so on. He used to say, "Farming is my culture. It is my first love. It is my breath." He used to say pointing at his labourers, "Working in the field is an interesting play for all of us." His approach towards his work caused a manifold growth in the yield. Naturally, it gave a financial stability to our family and those of the labourers working in our field.

The case of my second brother was different. He hated working in the field and getting his clothes soiled, but he had a deep passion for the trade of agricultural yield. Since childhood, he used to accompany our father to the weekly market in our village to sell vegetables, fruits and grains in our farm. He was a great helping hand to our father. In the course of time, he learnt many business tactics. When our father grew old, my brother took over the responsibility to go to the market. He fulfilled it with a great efficiency. Thus he was interested in trade and business. During school days, his Maths score was never impressive at all, but now he could deal in thousands of rupees within no time. Now he even exports the produce in our farm, not only to other states but even to other countries. He purchases the products from other farmers at reasonable price and exports the products abroad. He has set up two state-of-the-art offices in Mumbai. Young commerce graduates work for him. Two chartered accountants handle the financial aspects of his business. He proudly tells us all, "The secret of my fitness is my being occupied with business."

I, however, was neither interested in farming nor in trade. Therefore, I chose to get educated. I enjoyed my education as if I am playing a game of my interest. I always stood first or second in my school. I scored 100 percent in Maths. I stood first in our *tehsil* in my matriculation exam, and completed my graduation with first class. Studying, reading, writing, listening, thinking was never a burden for me. On the contrary, it is a joyful play for me. My brothers often tried to involve me in their farming and business; they tried to tempt me in several different ways. Yet, I was, and am, happily engrossed in my learning and teaching. It is the meaning of a happy life for me.

The insane priest in George Bernard Shaw's play *John Bull's Other Ireland* says, "An ideal nation is like a commonwealth. Work is like a play here and play itself is like life." A.N. Whitehead says in his book *The Aims of Education*, "If work is influenced by intellectual and moral perspective, it becomes joyous and all the fatigue and pains are forgotten. It is a blessing when we like our work as much as a play." Robert Frost, a famous poet, has explained that 'work should be like a play', saying, "Our work and our interest should become one. Even if my eyes are two, they both see the same thing. Similarly, my interest and my need should be one. When you like work as much as a play for some material reason, it is then you do good work for God and Future."

In brief, when a person likes his/her work as if it is a play, he/she starts doing it with loyalty and dedication. Later they realize they have the qualities they had never thought of. The methods of working and the grand success in case of me and my brothers became possible only because we regarded our works as an interesting play.

In this regard, Nari Rustomji has given a beautiful portrayal of Harold Deane in his book titled *Enchanted Frontiers*. Sir Harold was the former secretary of the State of Assam. He was an ideal administrator. Perfection in work was his only aspiration. He liked to work as if it is an interesting, joyful play. He always did his best so that his work would be excellent, while holding the highest position amongst the government servants in Assam. He never avoided, bypassed or skipped any issue just because it is complicated, troublesome or painful. He aimed for perfection in work and to achieve this aim, he used to work as if it is a play.

Aristotle, a great thinker, says, "When a person regards his/her work as interesting as a favourite play, he/she puts all the best qualities and capacities to use. Then the person feels the work interesting like a play and he/she can reach the peak of happiness and contentment."

Huizinga, a renowned Dutch historian, has presented his theory of work: "Play is omnipresent. A business can be turned into a play and a play can be turned into a business. Healthy and amicable competition turns work into play."

Summing up: May a work be trivial or important, liking it as an interesting play is the best sign of contentment in life. A person is free, independent while playing. Similarly, if you regard your work as a play, you can be highly innovative.

***

18. EQUILIBRIUM OF WORK AND REST

Principle: Rest is as important as consistency in work. A balance of these two leads to the effectiveness of work.

Explanation: The relation between work and rest is complementary and nourishing to each other. A person's happiness in resting depends on how hard he/she works. The harder a person works, the more satiating is his rest. Once there was a rich builder who lived in his lavish house. He was suffering from insomnia. All the treatments failed, yet he could not experience a fast and undisturbed sleep. While being thus troubled by his insomnia, once he visited a remote village with some of his friends. They saw there some cowherds, farmers, fishermen and some other villagers working along a serene riverbank. In the blazing afternoon sun, some of them were enjoying a nap on the lush green grass. They had only a jute bag as a bed. They enjoyed the company of the vivacious flow of the river. Fishermen were humming a tune while engaged in fishing. Farmers and labourers had taken a lunch break, and were resting under shady trees after enjoying their simple meals. Even the cattle were happily chewing cud under the cool shade of trees. The insomniac builder becomes restless to see all this.

He asks a resting couple, "How can you rest here so calmly despite having no bed or anything else?" They answered, "Sir, we get so tired while working in the farm that we fall asleep the moment we lie down." The builder had got the message correct. He and his friends asked some other people, "You don't have any means of entertainment here, right?" "Not at all, Sir! These tall green trees, cheerful flow of the river, carefree cattle grazing on hilltops, cowherds playing melodious tunes on their flutes… If you see around, we need no other means of entertainment. We fall fast asleep as soon as we go to bed. We get up with the cheery chirping of birds." This delightful response of the villager was an eye-opener for the insomniac builder. He realized that tiresome physical hardwork, carefree happy lifestyle in the company of nature is the panacea for his insomnia. This is the reason why Nature is called the best teacher, guide and doctor.

But how can we, addicted to the hollow materialism, unrestrained enjoyments and meaningless entertainment, understand the value of hardwork and subsequent rest? It is high time to introspect in which direction we are progressing in this techno-savvy era. Development and change are undoubtedly needed, but they should not be destructive and devastating. A great philosopher/ thinker Bertrand Russell used to walk forty miles on a holiday. He says, "I experience bliss in sitting quietly after I take such a long walk. I need nothing else." Mahatma Gandhi used to walk 10-12 kilometers a day. Swami Vivekananda used to travel on foot. He used to retire early at night and wake up early to do his chores. If we look back in the history, we can learn that Gautam Buddha and his disciples used to walk for miles. They used to halt to educate people wherever necessary. They used to take rest in humble places like a shady tree or simply on the ground. Many such examples of the equilibrium of work and rest can be found.

If one wants to enjoy his resting time, he has to do a lot of hard work. The person who does his routine work – may it be mechanical or monotonous – with loyalty and perfection, he can experience the true joy of rest. He can sleep well during night. On the contrary, a lazy person who evades work would have to suffer from insomnia. If a person avoids working wholeheartedly, it is harmful not only for him alone but also for his family and the organization where he works.

Therefore, the key to enjoy the pure joy of rest is to work till you get exhausted. Bernard Shaw says, "Work is not a part of life; work itself is life. Because it is work that gives meaning to life. Work is the foundation of our life." Work shapes the activities in our life. It makes our life well-managed and disciplined. All of us know the meaning of the saying 'An empty mind is a devil's workshop.' If there is no work, there will only be anarchy and unrest.

Rest is a requisite after hard work. It gives happiness, energy and boost. However, relaxation beyond certain limit has exactly opposite effect. Too much relaxation, lack of work and a tendency to evade work awakens the devil in mind, and the person may get addicted to bad habits. Naturally, the person recedes into darkness and also affects those around him.

Summing up: The conscientious, inspiring and uplifting equilibrium of work and rest is very essential.

***

19. THE UNIVERSE OF WORK

Principle: The universe of work is relative for a person, a family and an organization.

Explanation: The universe of work is a vast expanse full of diversity. It is captivating as well as marvelous. Just as the horizon keeps expanding when you reach higher and higher peaks, the work and its nature keeps expanding after reaching new levels. Judgment of work is absolutely beyond comprehension. Of course, it is relative for every individual, family and organization. But life without work is definitely unimaginable. Work gives meaning to a person's life. The universe of Work functions each moment of time, all day and night. If a sensible person thinks about how many works go on in the world, he will understand the great variety and types of works. Also, he will understand how one work is linked with the other. The universe of Work is unfathomable, because there can be innumerable works of trivial or important nature. This universe continuously undergoes changes, transformation and development.

The prism of work is multi-coloured and multi-dimensional. Human needs and emotions are varied. These needs can be fulfilled and feelings can be satiated only through work. Every living being, including animals and birds, has to work for fulfilling the basic needs. For instance, they need to work to collect their food and building or finding their shelters. Work can be of both sorts: highly significant or very trivial. This chapter discusses the factors like the universe of work, quality of work, values, their importance and so on.

It is necessary to know the purpose and nature of the work we are doing. Without knowing the purpose and nature of work, you just 'get tired' in vain. Such work cannot achieve development of an individual and of those who depend upon him.

A person can make progress and be happy in life only by proving his efficiency and using innovative ideas in work. Therefore, doing a work as a 'mandate' is meaningless. There is a well-known saying which means 'He perishes who stops'. That's why a person should be passionate about working well and maintaining its quality. A person who gives highest priority to Work is seldom miserable. On the contrary, a person who refrains from work gets nothing but misery. He also becomes a cause of miseries to those who depend on him. Most people in this world need to work for earning their daily bread and butter. If everyone has adequate work to do and if they are doing it well, it becomes the haven of peace and order. But, if people are devoid of work, a hell of turbulence and unrest is born there. This is the reason why the issue of unemployment is as explosive as a volcano. It is necessary to prioritise creating new and innovative jobs.

Abraham Maslow, the father of Humanitarian Psychology, said that "the universe of Work is too vast, deep and dynamic. Work is necessary for development and transformation. Work is an inseparable part of an individual's personality. It can be understood through work only." He studied and contemplated over psychological disorders, throughout his life. Finally, he gave up the idea that psychiatric treatment can cure a person. Man is always in search of happiness, but he cannot get it without work. Hence, Maslow eventually says, "A human being can attain salvation through doing the work his is destined to do, or is assigned to do, or that is neccessary to be done, using the best of his abilities." This succinct discussion can establish the importance of work and vastness of the universe of work.

Summing up: A person's world is as big as his brain. If this saying is considered in case of Work, one thing will be clear: Though work is immeasurable and varied in nature, it depends on the grasping ability of the concerned individual.

***

20. VALUE OF WORK

Principle: Here, value of work is not in terms of money. It suggests a very different thing. Let's understand it.

Explanation: Everyone needs to work to earn money. In fact, it is expected that your work should be everything for you. A person should think in such a way that his work will satisfy him as well as others. Every work done with a dedication, gives a joy of innovation. Aperson having infinite love and loyalty towards work can do something innovative. On the other hand, a person who is not interested in work performs a low-quality work, merely out of compulsion. Hence it is necessary to cultivate a habit of value-oriented work.

Self-satisfaction in work: Working for self-satisfaction, considering it as your own, is the highest value. An example can illustrate this well. There was a skilled worker who worked for a reputed building contractor. He used to build beautiful houses for the builder, who could earn a very good profit out of it. After many years of service, the worker began to feel like retiring from the job and spend his remaining life quietly with his family. He shared his thought with his boss, the builder. But he was not ready to let go a skilled worker like him. "Sir, please let me spend my remaining days of life with my family," he requested to his boss. Eventually his boss conceded to his request. But he put forth a condition: "Build one last house; then I shall free you from your job." Finally the worker accepted this condition.

However, he was not working for this last house with the same enthusiasm, involvement and dedication that he had for the earlier jobs. He worked on this house merely out of compulsion. He did not use the best quality material, nor did he pay heed to excellence and beauty while designing the house. He was only concerned about finishing this task at the earliest and get retired. He called his boss after finishing the job. The boss came with a lock and key for the new house. The worker showed the house to the boss. The latter said, "You have shown a great loyalty and integrity while working for me in all these years. I could earn a good reputation because of you. I earned a lot of money. I wish to give this house to you as a reward of your work. Please accept it." Saying this, the builder placed the lock and key in the worker's hand, and left after bidding him a loving goodbye.

The worker was stunned; he kept staring at the lock and key in his hand. He slumped down on the steps of the house that he had got as a reward. He thought, "If I knew that I am going to get this house in reward, I would have used better quality material, I would have been more careful about its designing. But…" Alas! Now these thoughts were pointless. He sat there in dejection. This is why every work should be done as if it is our own. The values such as affinity and involvement are important in every work. It is the value that adds quality to the work.

There was a landlord in a village. He was very kind hearted and amiable. Some men and women worked for him as labourers. They used to 'show' that they were involved in the work, but in the landlord's absence, they used to evade work. At times they used to steal vegetables and fruits in his farm. There was a poor tribal couple who used to tell these workers to stay away from such malpractices. But the lazy workers used to threaten the couple, "If you tell any of this to the landlord, we will eliminate you and your children." Afraid of these threats, the couple never told anything to the landlord.

However, the clever landlord observed all this. One day, he called all his servants, including the tribal couple. He paid the salary to the lazy workers and dismissed them. On the other hand, he gave a piece of land to the tribal couple as a reward for their honesty, where they could work and earn enough money for their well-being. The landlord also accepted the responsibility of educating their children. After all, it is rightly said that 'Honesty is the best policy.' Honesty is the highest value in the work. It is repaid definitely, in some or other way.

Nowadays we easily get carried away by advertisements. It is said about marketing that you can sell even rags by wearing gold, but you can't sell gold if you are wearing rags. However, it cannot be true in long term. Eventually what proves beneficial is quality, standard and utility of the work. You cannot cheat anyone twice. The quality and standard of work should not have reverse proportion with its growth or expansion. On the contrary, it should increase in proportion. Violating or neglecting the values in work is ultimately harmful for all. The development and progress is based on compromises and corruption is only a façade. It is reflected through instances like the falling bridges within a few years of construction, bursting dams, infertile seeds, ineffective fertilizers, things of below-standard weight, so on and so forth. Mahatma Gandhi has stated Seven Sins, among which there is a sin called Commerce without Morality. How many people are indulged in this sin, in the very own country of Mahatma Gandhi? We need to follow his teaching. These and such instances only cause devastation to not only the family but also the nation. The seven sins told by Mahatma Gandhi can indicate how important it is to nourish morality in work: 1) Politics without Principles, 2) Wealth without Work, 3) Pleasure without Conscience, 4) Knowledge OR Education without Character, 5) Commerce without Morality, 6) Science without Humanity, and 7) Worship or prayer without Sacrifice.

Destruction of work in various fields, man-made calamities, lack of quality in production, false weight, short life of products, collapsing roads, reduction in export, subsequent increase in unemployment— 'Work without Values' lies at the root of all this.

Summing up: It is for the ultimate good and welfare of all that we should nourish and worship core values of life in every work, so that we can get happiness, satisfaction and pleasure.

21. PRINCIPLES IN WORK

Principle: Work devoid of principles and quality is harmful for all.

Explanation: Everyone has to work; however, the work should be firmly rooted in values and a system of principles. Only then the work can be effective. A frame of ethics and principles makes the work fruitful. If the work has to be done, if it is a mandate, you can achieve a desired impact if you do it with an adherence to certain principles. Let's discuss some of the principles in brief.

1. **Undaunted spirit**: You may encounter failures while working. Failures are like speed breakers. It is important to keep working ceaselessly. It is possible that the pace of work may reduce, but you have to keep going ahead without getting frustrated. There are many inspiring stories to prove this point. Some of them are included at the end of this book.

2. **Consistency**: Many people are 'short-couraged', i.e. they are enthusiastic about a work only in the beginning. They suddenly develop interest in a work and start it. But they do not give a comprehensive thought to it. They start the work with excitement, but when they realise the complexity and problems, their excitement and enthusiasm ebbs. They become inconsistent. At times, they simply give up the work. They can achieve absolutely nothing, except wasting their energy.

3. **Modernity**: Many people are habitual to go by beaten pathways; they use only tried and tested methods of work, not thinking out of the box. It is true that one should not break the framework of ideals, principles and values. However, if some modern ways and techniques are available which can bring ease, simplicity, coherence and convenience, one should definitely adopt them with an open mind. Out-dated/ obsolete

thoughts and methods should be avoided. Creativity, passion for innovation, research and dynamic mind brings a lot of changes in work. This modernity in work needs to be accepted. The only thing to consider is that while accepting modernity, one should never give up quality, standard and values involved in the work.

4. **Inclusive attitude**: Everyone has some or other intention while working, which is perfectly natural. But the intention should not be a selfish one. The work should not be inspired by selfish desire of earning undue profit, exploiting others and accumulating more and more material wealth. A sense of social commitment, duty and conscience should be there in everything we do. There are several reputed brands in the world that have worked and are working with a purpose of earning appropriate profit and maintaining their standards of quality.

5. **Audit and observation**: This is a highly important principle in work. There are instances of companies who have withdrawn their ready products from market after they encountered the flaws in them. Some reputed companies/ manufacturers recall such faulty products, or offer to repair or replace them, even after they reach customers. It is only through audit and observation that they come to know their own errors and flaws. This is an essential principle in every small or big task.

6. **Sensitivity**: Work done with sensitivity gives pleasure. On the contrary, a work done insensitively gives nothing but pain. That's why it is said that the relation between work and worker should be like a mother-child relationship. Maternal feeling for work is serene. A mother can instantly know if something is wrong with her child. It is her sharp sensitivity that is at work here. Similarly, there should be such maternal affinity for work. It has to be so, since it is what brings perfection, excellence and best quality to the work.

Summing up: Success of a work depends on the inclusion of the above principles in it. They lead to transformation, progress and holistic development.

***

INSPIRING STORIES

We get to hear many cases of corruption. Even the people who wallow in riches are seen to be engaged in corruption. They blatantly tell lies to collect more and more wealth, and kill all the morality in work. On such a backdrop, we feel surprised to hear and read about common people who work diligently and sincerely. Here are some inspiring tales:

1. I know an auto-rikshaw driver. He never takes a rupee more than the amount indicated by meter. It feels very safe to travel in his auto even late at night. If a passenger forgets his valuables in his auto, he returns it to the owner very sincerely. He plays melodious songs in his auto. His auto is always clean and neat. Once I casually asked him, "Do you earn enough money in this business?" He said, "Sir, we are a small family of four. I am free from any addiction. We have no liking for any cheap pleasures. God gives us enough to fulfil our needs. He has never kept us hungry." He folded his hands in reverence for God. I learnt that if we add sincerity to our accepted work, we can live happily and contentedly.

2. The outcome of our work is determined by our feeling for it. Two magicians used to perform their magic shows in a reputed five-star hotel. However, both the magicians performed with a completely different feeling. One felt, "Today I am going to entertain people a lot. I am going to satisfy them. I am going to show the best of my skills and expertise." Feeling thus, he used to perform his magic show which would be really enthralling. People used to enjoy it a lot, and forget their worries and problems. His magic show was a miraculous remedy for them.

    On the contrary, the other magician behaved very differently. He was a cheater by habit. He could barely manage to perform the show somehow. Naturally, he used to earn less than the first one. The first magician received invitations of shows from many places. That's why, it is rightly said, 'As you sow, so shall you reap.'

3. We should always look for innovation in any work. New ideas and methods should be tried in order to make progress. In line with this very principle, a psychologist created five small rooms in his house and left a rat in a room where he had kept some sweets. The rat went to the fifth room and simply ate away the sweets. After three days, the scientist kept the sweets in the third room. Firstly, the rat went straight to the fifth room where he could not find sweets and was disappointed not to find anything there. He then went to the fourth room, but in vain. Then he went to the third room, where he was rejoiced to find sweets. He searched other rooms as well, and found the sweets. The psychologist says, "we humans do not easily break up with the set methods, despite having sharp intellect." Change and transformation are the inevitable parts of work. Generally, the people with complacent, conventional attitude do not tend to change the rigid framework of their routine. They are reluctant to search for the sweets of innovation. Naturally, their progress and development comes to a standstill. It is said, "Fear is a dark room where only negatives are developed." Fear gives birth to pessimism. Hence, it is desirable to have fearlessness, security and safety in work. It is what can lead to transformation and development.

4. A work of collective importance should always be done by two, two hundred, two thousand hands… the essence of this sentence highlights the importance of teamwork. Once, Swami Vivekananda's speech was organised for young boys and girls. The topic was: Organisation/ teamwork (संघटन). Many youngsters were waiting for Swamiji in a big hall. As he arrived, the audience gave a huge applause to welcome him. When the applause subsided and the audience became quiet,

Swamiji cast a loving glance upon them and said, "Today I have fallen in love with 'one'." All the people in the audience were stunned. Who might be this celestial beauty that a handsome guy like Swamiji has fallen in love with? People started glancing towards each other with questions in eyes. Observing this, Swamiji clarified without stretching their curiosity, "It is Organisation/ teamwork." Once again, there was a huge applause filled with admiration. Later, Swamiji talked for next one hour about the importance of teamwork in accomplishing any big task.

5. Here is a story that will inspire you to maintain quality and standard of work. LokmanyaTilak was in jail when he received the news that his son has passed his board exams with the first rank. As soon as he received this news, he wrote a letter to his son from the prison, "Dear Son, first of all, I congratulate you from the bottom of my heart. Never ask me the question, 'Where should I seek admission, *Baba*?' Do what you like a lot and what is right according to your conscience. But whatever you do, immerse yourself in it. Whatever field you choose, give only your best. It doesn't matter even if you sell shoes. But do it so well that people should say, 'You want to buy shoes? Go to Tilak's shop.' You should earn such goodwill/trust through your work."

6. A feeling of optimism is very important in any work. It is this optimism that makes the work successful, even before starting the work. This incident in the life of Thomas Alva Edison can inspire you in this regard. He was experimenting relentlessly to invent an electric bulb. 999 of his experiments failed, and it was 1000th experiment that turned successful, and he invented the electric bulb. Edison said about his tireless work, "My 999 experiments did not fail. On the contrary, those 999 experiments proved that they are not the correct ways to make an electric bulb. My efforts were not wasted. They inspired me to find new ways."

7. It is believed that a mission should be started on some auspicious time/moment. It has, although, no scientific evidence. King Harshavardhan was famous for his valour. He used to go on war campaigns frequently in order to expand his empire. Once, while starting a campaign, a ring in his finger dropped in the mud on the ground. Soldiers saw it as a serious ill omen. The king showed the mud-covered ring to the dejected, depressed soldiers, and said, "Just like this ring has left it's imprint on the muddy ground, your valour will leave its imprint on the land you conquer." The soldiers got a boost to see this optimistic inspiring energy of the king. Needless to say, they were victorious in the campaign.

8. King Harshavardhan owned a lame elephant. He was lame for many years. All sorts of treatments went in vain on the elephant. When the king met Gautam Buddha, he shared with him about the lameness of the elephant. Buddha advised the king to change the *mahout* of the elephant. The king did so, and surprisingly, the elephant started walking normally within a few days. The king asked Buddha in astonishment the reason of this change. Buddha said, "This elephant was imitating his *mahout*. His *mahout* was lame, that's why the elephant walked as if he was lame too." There should not be blind imitation in case of any work. Pragmatic approach and growth-oriented thinking is very important.

9. If you are ready to give up your stagnancy and the habit of treading only known routes, you can easily attain happiness, satisfaction and contentment using this vision and attitude. Following fable can explain it better: A shepherd had three sheep. He used to make them graze in dry grassland. There was area of green grassland beyond ten feet. Since the shepherd did not want his sheep to go there, he bought three ropes of ten feet each, and tied the sheep with the rope. First sheep goes till four-five feet. But she strips off the rope and comes back to her original place. The second one imitates her,

though she manages to go a little more distance. But the third one doesn't pay attention to them, and keeps going ahead. When she reaches the tenth foot, the rope around her neck jerks her back. But the sheep focuses on the green grass. Determining to get it, she jerks ahead. Finally her efforts are successful, and the rope is cut, making the sheep free. She starts running till she reaches the eleventh feet and relishes the green grass. The first two sheep cannot relish the green grass because they are complacent with the dry grass they get. They do not take any efforts to reach the green grass.

10. A person should have an open mind while doing any work. Mind should not be prejudiced. It should be free from vices like anger, greed, jealousy, ego etc. When mind is clear, clean and free, you can get a true happiness of self-actualisation from work. The incident mentioned below is certainly inspiring. Once I was delivering a lecture on the topic Work Culture. In the beginning of the lecture, I showed my handkerchief to the audience and asked, "Tell me the uses of this handkerchief." Various answers came from the audience: wiping hands, nose, placing it before face while sneezing, placing it on head in the hot sun etc. Then I tied two knots to the handkerchief, and asked, "Can we use this handkerchief now? Can we wipe hands to it? Can we tie it on our head or face?" 'No.' A collective answer came from the audience. I spoke further. "When the handkerchief was free, it had many uses. But now that it has knots, it is of no use. Similarly, any work should be done with an open mind. A parachute is useful only when you open it. If it is not opened, you will meet the end of your life. Don't let it happen in case of work."

11. It is said that 'Work is worship.' When a devotee worships his God, he forgets himself. The same should happen in case of work. When Shri Swami Samarth lived in Akkalkot during 1857 to 1878, there was a blacksmith named Maruti. He used to work very honestly and diligently to earn his bread and

butter. Before starting work, he used to come to bow before Swami. He would do the same even at the end of the day's work.

His wife, Kashibai, used to assist him in his work. She would chant Swami's name while working. Maruti used to beat the hot iron and make tools from it. However, some vagabonds in Akkalkot used to tell Swami, "*Maharaj*, that Maruti is always engrossed in his work. He doesn't understand that the God Himself resides in Akkalkot in your form." Swami used to scold them, "He sees God in his work. And you come here only to eat." Saint Sawata Mali could not go to Pandharpur to see Lord Vitthal. Instead, he used to work in his farm and say, "My vegetables are my Vitthal." Saints like Sena Maharaj, Gora Kumbhar used to see God in their work itself.

12. Diligence, sincerity, promptness, firmness and modesty lead to the growth off business. Here is a story that speaks of these virtues. I know an auto driver named Raghu. While giving service to anyone, he charges as per meter only. His lifestyle is very simple and neat. He speaks very sweetly and modestly. He plays soothing music in his auto. He never uses abusive words. He is so trustworthy that anyone – young and old, men and women alike – can safely travel in his auto any time. Many retired officers, reputed people call him only. They have his cell phone number. They wait till he comes. He has a good judgment of his customers. That's why he sometimes even refuses to some customers. If a passenger forgets some valuables or documents in his auto, and if Raghu knows their address or number, he returns those things to their owners and doesn't accept a single penny in reward. Most of the times his auto is already booked. Where does it come from?

13. There should not be egoistic approach in working or getting any work done. Egoism is the feeling of being the 'doer', protecting the workers, patronising them, and being high on such feeling. Here is a story that tells you not to have such

feelings. Once, a king and his *Guru* were sitting under a mango tree on a vast open ground. Hundreds of the king's soldiers were busy with their works in the ground. Looking at them, the king thought egoistically, 'I am the one who provides bread and butter to so many soldiers and their families.' The king's *Guru* sensed the expression of ego on the king's face. He pointed at a huge rock in front of them and asked the king to get it moved aside. As soon as the rock was moved, a frog jumped from below the rock. The *Guru* asked pointing at the frog, "I suppose you provide for this frog as well?" The king startled to realise the ego that was aroused in his mind some time before. He realised his mistake and asked for forgiveness.

14. Any work should not be done blindly, and using the set method. It is important to keep updated knowledge and pragmatic attitude. Evaluation of your work is based on how expertly and skilfully you do it. A story of a fruit vendor is enlightening in this regard. He used to sell apples on his handcart. He placed a board on his cart: Apples Rs.100/ kg. He visited everywhere in the village, shouting the price of apple, but he couldn't find a single customer to buy 1 kg apple for Rs. 100 or more. Everyone bargained with him, no one gave a single rupee more to him.

15. Any work should not be done in old-fashioned, dogmatic and monotonous way. It does not lead to change and transformation. It is necessary to expand the range of one's thoughts and perspective. Else, you cannot make progress. A farmer's story can tell you how dogmatism is harmful. The farmer had grown pumpkins in his farm. One day, just for fun, he put a glass vessel around a small pumpkin on the creeper. When he plucked ripe pumpkins after some days, he realised that all other pumpkins had grown big, but the pumpkin inside the glass vessel had remained as small as the size of vessel. The vessel had limited the growth capacity of pumpkin.

16. Fear while working causes secretion of negative and frightening hormones in the body which in turn affect the work. Fear does not let you achieve desired success. You might fail. The following story shows this principle. A man was sentenced to death for some crime. It was going to be a death by snake-bite. A snake was brought before the person. He knew the method of his death sentence. His eyes were tied, and instead of the snake, two sharp pins like snake's teeth were pricked into his skin. Yet, he felt that the snake had bitten him, and many frightening secretions took place in his body, which actually had their effect like a snake's poison. Fear created in him the symptoms of snake-bite and he died. Thus it is harmful to develop such fear in a person.

17. If you get an enthusiastic and optimistic ambience while working, it enhances the speed, quality and productivity of the work. A psychologist explained this through an example. A war elephant got trapped in a marshy ground. He could not come out despite taking lot of efforts. Eventually, he remained trapped in the marsh. His *mahout* made many attempts to take him out, but all in vain. Gautam Buddha was passing from there with his disciples. The *mahout* told him what had happened with the war elephant. Gautam Buddha listened to him and told, "Create a warlike atmosphere around where the elephant is trapped. Play battle drums." People did so, and the elephant dragged himself up with all his energy to go forward as if in a battle. The elephant had a tremendous energy to fight, to come out of the mud. The warlike ambience simply awakened his power. Hence, the feeling of vigilance and assured victory leads one to success.

18. Positive, well-intended criticism should be accepted open-mindedly. But we can neglect jealous, derogatory criticism and go ahead. Henry Ford, the father of automobiles industry, is the best example of this. He brought his first crude model of automobile on the streets of Detroit. He had to face a lot of

criticism for it. People used to deride him and his vehicle. But Henry was firm. He kept making changes in the model to refine and develop it. One day, he became a successful businessman in the automobile industry. He earned reputation as well as wealth, and became famous all over the world as the father of automobile industry.

19. Work should never be affected by ideas like auspicious-inauspicious or good-ill omens. Here is a story that suggests this principle. Napoleon Bonaparte was a phenomenal warrior, who used to organise various war campaigns and conquer new lands. Once he called his soldiers on the seashore to prepare for such a war campaign in a new land. All soldiers gathered there according to his orders. When Napoleon was alighting from the ship, he slipped and fell on his face. His chest was covered in mud. The superstitious soldiers became anxious. They felt that the defeat is assured in this campaign since their leader fell down. They felt defeated even before the war. However, the invincible Napoleon regained his posture and said to his soldiers, "My brave soldiers, we are going to definitely win this battle, because I have embraced this land the moment, I set foot here. She has as if promised me that she will be mine only." And he did really win the battle.

20. When you work for an organisation, company or a firm, or for a businessman or shopkeeper, have positive, respectful, pragmatic and transformational thoughts for the owner or the concerned person or organisation. It is beneficial for you as well as for those who you work for. Understand the moral of the following story: A king was going somewhere with his retinue, when a man was coming from the opposite side of the same road. The king angrily pointed at him, and ordered his soldiers to arrest him and throw him in jail. The soldiers immediately obeyed. Next day, the Prime Minister asked the king about reason to arrest the man. The king said, "I cannot tell any specific reason, but when I saw that man, my anger

knew no bounds, and I simply gave an order to imprison him. Now it's upto you what you make of it." The righteous Prime Minister went to the jail and interrogated that man. The prisoner started begging forgiveness, "I don't know why the king gave this punishment to me, but I am in dire need of money for my daughter's wedding. I don't have enough money. But I have a pile of sandalwood. Now who would buy such expensive sandalwood? While thinking so, I saw the king. I thought, "If the king dies, the sandalwood pyre would be needed. Then my sandalwood will be sold out." The same instant, the king ordered to arrest me." The Prime Minister understood what had happened. When the man had such negative thoughts for the king, their eyes met and a feeling of anger was aroused. Hence, the psychologists rightly say, "Brain and heart are the roots of every activity."

21. Many people in this world have withstood failure and have become successful through their persistence and perseverance. We should recall such examples from time to time, and then get ready to work. We call it 'charging the battery of mind'. Abraham Lincoln, the 16th President of United States of America, exemplifies it well. At the age of 21, he suffered a great loss in his business. At 22, he lost the parliamentary election. At 24, once again he suffered a business loss. When he was 26, his wife passed away at such a young age. At 27, he was depressed. At 34, he again lost the parliamentary elections. At 45, he lost Senate elections. At 47, he lost an opportunity to be the Vice-President. At 49, he again lost the Senate elections. Eventually, at 52, he won the presidential elections.

22. A village had become deserted due to the troubles created by a monster called Goliath. The frightened villagers came to David, the shepherd. David told them, "The monster is too big to run fast. We need not have a perfect aim to kill him. If we all throw stones and arrows at him, they will certainly hit

somewhere on his huge body." Later, the villagers did so, and the monster was killed. If you assess the long-term risks and act accordingly, you can certainly become successful. This is an important piece of teaching.

23. The owner of a shoe factory did some injustice to the workers. Although the workers wanted justice, they did not stop the work. They continued their work, but manufactured only the right leg shoes. When their just demands were fulfilled, they manufactured the left leg shoes, and completed their task. Without stopping work, the workers compelled the owner to deliver justice. After their demands were fulfilled, they completed the remaining work. Consequently, it did not cause any loss to the owner as well. Thus, work has to be continued with a perspective towards the greater good.

24. A tiny living being like ant keeps working every moment. On the contrary, a human being, in spite of being endowed with all capabilities, is lazy and skips his work. He feels work a burden. He forgets the saying that means, 'God resides in hard work'.

25. Around 3500 experiments conducted by a scientist failed. Still, he used to get up early every morning to resume his experiments.

26. Mahatma Gandhi's daily routine was very meticulous and punctual. Despite the political opposition, differences of opinion and derision, he never let his scheduled works get disturbed.

27. Swami Vivekananda once told an audience of youth, "Even if you have faith in thirty-three crores gods, but not in yourself and your accepted work, then you are an atheist."

28. Swami Vivekananda's prayer for optimism in work: "O God, give me the strength of changing what I can change in this world. Give me the capacity of adjust with what I cannot change. Give me the wisdom to distinguish between what I can change and what I cannot, while working."

29. It is important a concrete goal while working, so that you can achieve success. For instance, Laxmanrao Kirloskar, the founder of Kirloskar Industries, was a humble drawing teacher in a school. He founded a group of industries on a barren expanse of land. Dhirubhai Ambani was a clerk at a petrol pump and earned merely Rs. 300 as salary. But relentless and goal-oriented hard work made him a great businessman who gave jobs to lakhs of people. Dr. A.P.J. Abdul Kalam became a great scientist by working very hard since his childhood. Later he became the President of India, and was also awarded Bharat Ratna, the highest civilian award of India.

APPENDIX

- Fraser, Ronald (Ed.). *Work*, Volume
- Galbraith J.K. *The New Industrial state*
- Herzberg F. *Work and the Nature of Man.*
- Huizinga Johan – *Home Ludens.*
- Lorenz, Konrad. *Civilzed Man's right Deadly sins.*
- Lorenz, konrad. *On Aggression.*
- Malcolm, Norman – Ludwig Wittgenstein.
- Maslow, Abraham H. Eupsychian – *Management.*
- McClelland, David C. and Winter. Dadid G. Motativating *Economic Achievement.*
- McClelland, David C. *The Achieving Society.*
- Mikes, George. *The Land of the Rising Yen.*
- Schumacher, E.F. *Small is Beautiful.*
- Whitenead A.N. – *The Aims of Education.*
- Patil, Dr. Yashwantrao. *Sanskaracha Amritkalash.* Vishwakarma Prakashan, pune.
- Sapre, S. A. *Apale Kam, Apale Jeevan-Sarvasva.* National Book Trust of India.

ABOUT THE AUTHOR

1. Name   : Pr. Dr. Yashwantrao Shankarrao Patil

2. Nationality   : Indian

3. Address   : 13, 'Rajas' Bungalow, Tidke Colony, Opp. Raunak Apartment, Near Mico Circle, C/O Yashwant Classes, Tidke Colony Branch, Nashik 422 003 (0253)23142278.

4. Office Address : Yashwant Classes, Gajanan Enclave, Ashok Stambh, Gangapur Road, Nashik-1. Phone- (0253) 6455388. Cell phone- 9890615649. Email- yashwantraopatil1947@rediffmail.com

5. Education   : B.A. (Hon.) L.L.B., Ph.D. (Marathi) from Pune University.

6. Occupation   : Teacher, Farmer, Lecturer

7. Hobbies : Reading, travelling, writing.

   Founder editor of a weekly magazine 'Lok Ankush' and monthly magazine 'Marga Deep'.

   Writing published in various periodicals and newspapers on topics like agriculture, cooperation, spirituality, and personality portraits.

   Articles on dignified persons on the occasions of their birthdays in the memorial books on them.

8. Published Books

1. *English Essays for Std. X & XII*

2. *English Passages for Std. X & XII*

3. *English Grammar for Std. X & XII*

4. *Shri Swami Samarth Upasana Va Falashruti* (Second Edition)

5. *Shri Swami Samarthanchya Leelanchya Arthabodhachi Bakhar* (Second edition)

6. Shree Swaminchi Divyanubhuti (Based on Ph.D. thesis)

7. *Shree Swami Samarthanchya Faladayi Birudavalya*

8. *Jeevanache Adhyatma*

9. *Vedh Manacha, Shodh Sukhacha*

10. *Sanskarancha Amrutkalash*

11. *Tension Nako Abhyasache* (Keys to study)

12. *Nityache Sangati* (A recital book of four chapters) (Second Edition)

13. *Shri Swami Samarth Upasanechi Mule Va Fale* (Second Edition)

14. *Niramay Anandi Vardhakya*

15. *Ishwariya Samarthyache Mahameru Shri Swami Samarth*

16. *Rokhthok Sant Tukaram*

17. *Vicharanchya Chandanya*

18. *Sarvanchya Sarvangin Vikasasathi Adhyatmik Bodh-katha* (Vol 1 & 2)

19. Sant Tukaramanche "Rokh-Thok Vicha"

20. Gadhivarchya Aaisaheb (Novel)

21. Gandhalleli Fule (Katha Sangrah)

8. Upcoming Books

1. Book based on the thesis on Shri Swami Samarth (Vol 2) (*Shri Swami Samarth: Achar-vichar, Dharma Va Tattvadnyan*)

2. *Preranechya Parambya*

3. *Adhyatmik Vikasachya Goshti*

4. *Adhyatmik Vikasasathi Preranadayi Goshti*

5. *Sansarvel* (novel)

6. *Sarvansathi Namasmaranache Mahattva*

7. *Preranadayi Vicharanchi Mandiyali*

8. *Parinamkari Sujan Palakatva*

9. *Palakneeti* (Vol 1 & 2)

10. *Ayushyavar Mahattvache Bolu Kahi*

11. *Adhyatmacha Dhoor, Dhurala, Darval*

12. *Corona che Mahabharat*

9. Other : Delivered lectures at Dr. Jaykar External Lecture Series of Pune University, Saint Gadage Maharaj Senior Citizen Lecture Series, and late Yashwantrao Chavan Lecture Series of Pune University

10. Writing:

- Forewords to the books by some other poets and writers, which were published mostly in the Weekly 'Lok Ankush'

- Participation in many seminars and discussions on books

- Hundreds of lectures delivered on various literary topics, on various occasions in many schools and colleges

- Active participation in the work of some organisations active in political, social, educational and spiritual fields

- Columns on the topics like spirituality, social work, politics, education, environment etc. in leading newspapers in Maharashtra

- Production of and a small role played in a Marathi film 'Attaracha Faya'

11. Awards: Awards by various organisations at tehsil, disctrict and State level.